INFANTRY SUPPORT WEAPONS

MORTARS, MISSILES AND MACHINE GUNS

GREENHILL MILITARY MANUALS

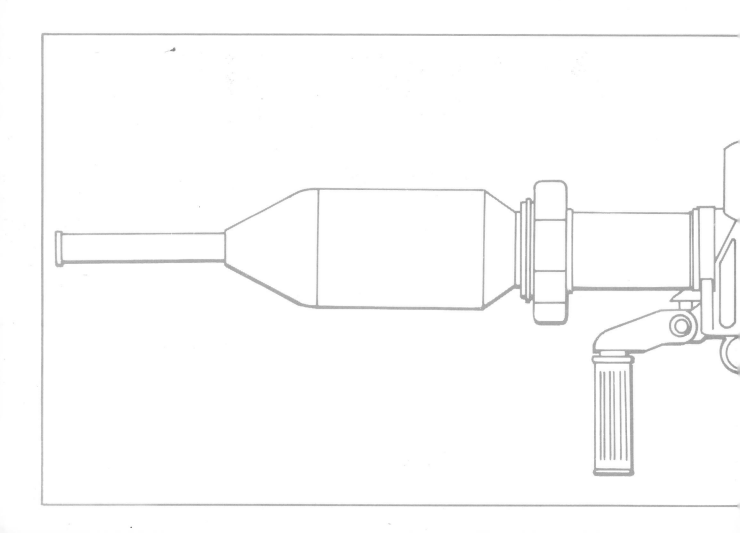

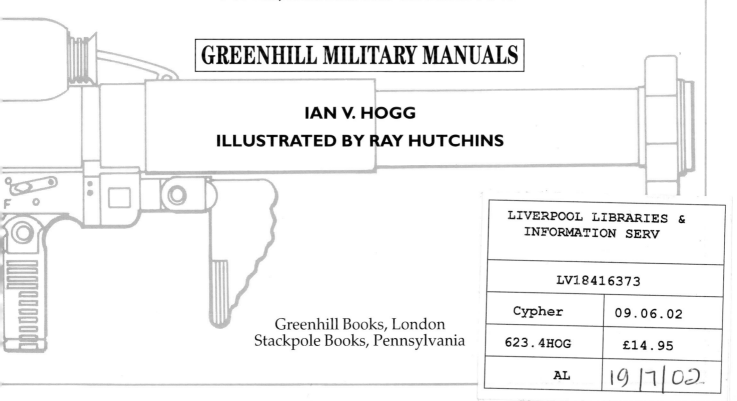

INFANTRY SUPPORT WEAPONS

MORTARS, MISSILES AND MACHINE GUNS

GREENHILL MILITARY MANUALS

IAN V. HOGG

ILLUSTRATED BY RAY HUTCHINS

Greenhill Books, London
Stackpole Books, Pennsylvania

This edition of
Infantry Support Weapons
first published 2002 by Greenhill Books, Lionel Leventhal Limited, Park House, 1 Russell Gardens, London NW11 9NN
and
Stackpole Books, 5067 Ritter Road, Mechanicsburg, PA 17055, USA

British Library Cataloguing in Publication Data
Hogg, Ian V. (Ian Vernon), 1926–
Infantry support weapons: mortars, missiles and machine guns. (Greenhill military manuals)
1. Weapons 2. Infantry – Equipment
I. Title
623.4

ISBN 1-85367-484-2

Library of Congress Cataloging-in-Publication Data available

Designed by Merlin Publications
Printed and bound in Singapore by Kyodo Printing Company

Introduction

The object of war is to bring the enemy's army to battle, defeat it, and occupy his country. Given this, it becomes apparent that the infantry are going to do most of the donkey-work, particularly the bit about occupying the country. Nothing convinces a population that it is beaten as much as the sight of an armed soldier in a strange uniform standing on the corner of his street. That being understood, it becomes obvious that everything which has contributed to putting that man on that street corner can be called an 'infantry support weapon'. Battleships, aircraft carriers, tanks, artillery, bombers, ballistic missiles... all, in the final analysis, are infantry support weapons. But I tend to think that there would be some tooth-sucking in many quarters if we were to include such articles in this book.

So this book is about what are commonly considered the support weapons; the ones which the infantry operate in order to provide firepower over and above that which they dispose with their personal weapons. Whilst the armour, artillery and tactical air are there to provide heavy support, there are frequent occasions when something less cumbersome and quicker needs to be applied in order to resolve a sudden problem. So the machine gun, the grenade launcher, the mortar, the anti-tank missile, and several other devices are carried along rather as a golf bag, and when the need arises the infantryman delves into the bag to produce the club needed to get him out of the rough.

It was not always thus; the proliferation of high-technology weapons for the infantry is something which began to appear during World War Two but which then languished for many years until suddenly taking wing once more in the middle 1970s. One reason for this has been the shrinking size of infantry forces; once upon a time the infantry conquered its enemies by manpower; now it requires technology to do the same job since the men are simply not there. The techno-speak for this is 'force multiplier' - the ability of a weapon system to provide the man with greater firepower and greater effectiveness in order to compensate for lack of numbers. Another reason is that targets have become more resistant and more dangerous, and thus they demand complex weapons with which they can be dealt with rapidly, before they can do their own 'force multiplying'. And, as the following pages will show, today's infantryman has a bewildering choice of weapons at his disposal.

Note that this does not set out to catalogue every weapon in the various categories; it merely shows some examples, which indicate the way that modern technology had moved over the past twenty years.

Contents

Introduction..5

The Future..8

Ameli 5.56 mm Machine Gun, Spain................10

Minimi 5.56 mm Machine Gun, Belgium................12

Ultimax 100 5.56 mm Machine Gun, Singapore........14

Negev 5.56 mm Light Machine Gun, Israel................16

MAG 7.62 mm Machine Gun, Belgium................18

M60 7.62 mm Machine Gun, USA................20

MG3 7.62 mm Machine Gun, Germany................22

PK 7.62 mm Machine Gun Family, F. Soviet Union.....24

Browning 50 in. M2HB Machine Gun, USA................26

Jackhammer Combat Shotgun, USA................28

Weapon Sights..30

FLY-K Weapon System, France................32

L9A1 51 mm Mortar, UK................34

Hirtenberger 60 mm Commando Mortar, Austria....36

ECIA 60 mm Commando Mortar, Spain................38

ECIA 60 mm Model L Mortar, Spain................40

Breda 81 mm Mortar, Italy................42

M3 81 mm Mortar, South Africa................44

L16 81 mm Mortar, UK................46

Hirtenberger M12-111 120 mm Mortar, Austria.......48

M74 120 mm Light Mortar, Yugoslavia................50

Hotchkiss MCB-81 81 mm Gun-Mortar, France....52

Strix Anti-tank Guided Mortar Projectile, Sweden....54

Bussard Anti-tank Guided Mortar, Germany................56

Merlin 81 mm Guided Mortar Projectile, UK................58

Ammunition..60

GLF-90 Multiple Grenade Launcher, Italy................62

CIS 40-AGL Auto. Grenade Launcher, Singapore.....64

Armscor MGL 6-shot Grenade Launcher,

S. Africa................66

GP-25 40 mm Grenade Launcher, F. Soviet Union....68

AGS-17 Grenade Launcher, F. Soviet Union................70

LAG-40 Automatic Grenade Launcher, Spain................72

RAAM, USA................74

Rifleman's Assault Weapon (RAW), USA 76

M203 Grenade Launcher, USA 78

Rifle Grenades 80

Milan Anti-tank Missile, France 82

Eryx Anti-tank Missile, France 84

Panzerfaust 3 Anti-tank Launcher, Germany 86

Folgore Anti-tank System, Italy 88

Apilas Anti-tank Launcher, South Africa 90

SAM-7 Strela AA Missile, F. Soviet Union 92

RPG-7 Anti-tank Launcher, F. Soviet Union 94

C-90-C Weapon System, Spain 96

AT-4 Anti-tank Launcher, Sweden 98

Carl Gustav M2 84 mm Recoilless Gun, Sweden 100

RBS-70 AA Missile, Sweden 102

Blowpipe AA Missile, UK 104

LAW 80 Anti-tank Launcher, UK 106

M72 66 mm Anti-tank Launcher, USA 108

Stinger AA Missile, USA 110

SMAW, USA 112

AT-8 Bunker Buster, USA 114

Superdragon Anti-tank Missile, USA 116

TOW 2 Anti-tank Missile, USA 118

Javelin AAWS/M, USA 120

Surveillance Equipment 122

Tarasque 20 mm AA Gun, France 124

ZPU 14.5 mm AA Machine Gun, F. Soviet Union 126

ZU 23 mm AA Cannon, F. Soviet Union 128

Diana 25 mm AA Cannon, Switzerland 130

M242 Chain Gun, USA 132

ASP 30 mm Cannon, USA 134

M18A1 57 mm Recoilless Rifle, USA 136

M40A1 106 mm Recoilless Gun, USA 138

M55A4B1 20mm Multiple AA Cannon,

Yugoslavia 140

Hand Grenades 142

Glossary 144

The Future

There is never any shortage of prophets ready to tell us what the infantryman of the 21st century will look like. If their prophecies are anything to go by, he will be nine feet tall and built like an Olympic wrestler; he'll have to be in order to carry everything the prophets want to hang on him! He will also need a degree in computer science, because every solution seems to be intent upon providing him with integrated helmet sights, a head-up display on a visor which overlays the right map on top of his view of the country, a radio data link which provides him with faxed order sheets, details of the enemy's dispositions, orders, demands for ration returns, statements of ammunition expenditure and who knows what else. He will be carrying a highly technical weapon which will instantly switchable from precision shooting at individual targets to area saturation with high explosives. He will be proofed against gas, bugs, weather and climate, and will be able to see equally well by day and by night. The one item of equipment which never seems to figure in these prophecies is a shovel!

Away with prophecies. Let us simply ask ourselves what the infantryman is supposed to do and what he needs in order to do it. After that we can ask what the technology can provide which will be of some practical value.

First, abandon any preconceptions you may have; today's infantryman is not a moron with a rifle in one hand and a shovel in the other. He is among the most highly trained and highly skilled of soldiers; as a glimpse at these pages will show, he has to be able to turn his hand to operating a wider variety of weapons than any other type of soldier, and at the same time he has to practice all the older skills such as fieldcraft, camouflage, target recognition, construction of defensive positions, signalling, basic cookery and so forth for a long list.

Forget also any weasel words such as 'imposing his will on the enemy'. The infantryman's job is to kill his enemy while avoiding being killed himself. To do that he needs weapons. He needs, first and foremost, a personal weapon with which to kill his opponents and defend himself. He needs longer-ranging weapons to deal with the enemy as far away as possible so as to reduce the danger to himself. He needs weapons tailored to specific targets so as to achieve the maximum effect against those targets. The following pages show what he has today; what will he have tomorrow?

In my view, in thirty years' time he will probably be using the same weapons, perhaps slightly improved, but basically the same because we have now reached a point in the technology curve where it flattens out and any small improvement in performance will have a disproportionate cost attached to it. Today it is cost which rules procurement, not tactical requirements. There is a saying in the weapons trade that the final ten percent of performance is sixty percent of the cost, and if you contemplate the ability of today's weapons, you must then ask whether it is worth upping the price by sixty percent in order to obtain a ten percent improvement in the performance. The answer is obvious.

This, though, does not prevent designers or soldiers having ideas. Designers are currently at work trying to make a personal weapon which will fire a lethal laser beam rather than a solid projectile; one advantage of this would be its velocity, that cf the speed of light, which would render aim-off for moving targets virtually redundant. But the technical problems are formidable - not least the problem of carrying round the source of power for such a device. Mounting it on a vehicle would perhaps solve that problem, and a suggested solution is illustrated here. But can you really call this a personal weapon?

Another proposal is to provide remote-controlled vehicles which will carry the weapons forward, rather than using men. A controller, sitting safely in a deep hole well to the rear will, by television and radio control, guide the weapon into a suitable firing position and open fire. Again, the expense would appear to argue against it; these devices would be vulnerable to enemy fire, and the radio control would be vulnerable to counter-measures. Both these problems can perhaps be solved by ingenious design, but one would require several devices for each operator and a major supply problem in getting them to where they were wanted.

There is, presently, much talk about developing 'non-lethal' weapons. This, in my view, is a contradiction in terms. We have already defined the object of war, and non-lethal weapons will not achieve it. Moreover, how can you be sure that if you go to war with non-lethal weapons that the other side isn't using very lethal ones? If you do defeat an enemy using non-lethal weapons, you are storing up trouble for the future, for you may be sure than an enemy humiliated by non-lethal weapons will be itching to have a return bout - and he won't be in a non-lethal frame of mind.

So, on the whole, I do not think we are about to see any sudden technological leap in infantry weapons. Improved materials - carbon fibre instead of steel barrels for mortars are currently being investigated, adding lightness to the man's load; better sights, with computing ability to iron out some of the many ballistic variations which reduce accuracy; cheaper manufacture by computer-controlled machinery; these are the minor improvements we will certainly see in the future. But no death-rays, no laser pistols, no atomic hand grenades.

Above: A proposal for a High Energy Laser system capable of operating as a weapon. Perhaps a future weapon, but not one which is likely to become small enough to be an infantryman's personal weapon.

Below: TMAP- the Tele-operated Mobile Anti-armour Platform. A remote-controlled vehicle which carries two rocket launchers and a cannon, guided by television cameras and controlled by radio or fibre-optic link. Several variations on this theme exist and they have their attractions. But cost isn't one of them.

AMELI 5.56 mm Machine Gun Spain

The **Ameli light machine gun** used by the Spanish Army looks very much like a scaled-down version of the German wartime MG42, and it does have a number of mechanical resemblances. However, the operating system is entirely different, even though it uses very similar parts.

The **Ameli** is a delayed blowback weapon, using the same roller locking system as that of the Spanish CETME Type L rifle and of the many Heckler & Koch rifles and machine guns, all of which owe their operating system to research carried on in Spain shortly after 1945. The bolt is in two parts, a light front and a heavier rear section which also carries the firing pin. These

two parts are kept separate by two rollers while the bolt is moving forward to chamber the cartridge. Once the cartridge is loaded, the front of the bolt stops; the rear of the bolt continues to move forward and forces the two rollers outwards into recesses in the receiver. This allows the rear of the bolt to move forward so that the firing pin strikes the cap and fires the cartridge. The breech pressure pushes the cartridge case back against the face of the bolt; this blow is transferred, via the rollers, to the rear body of the bolt, and at the same time the rearward movement begins to force the rollers out of their recesses and against the face of the rear section of the bolt. There is a mechanical leverage here

which drives the rear back faster than the front, so absorbing recoil energy. Once the rollers are clear of their recesses the entire bolt unit moves back as one piece, compresses a spring, ejects the spent case and then returns to load the next round.

The barrel can be quickly changed by simply unlocking the carrying handle and swinging it down, then pushing the barrel forward out of the receiver and pulling it out sideways. Feed is from a loose belt or from special disposable plastic 100 or 200-round belt boxes which clip to the left side of the gun. Normally fitted with a bipod, it can also be fitted to a tripod for sustained fire.

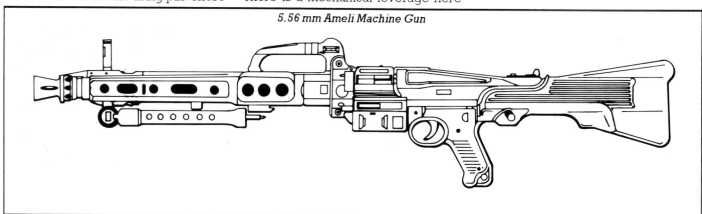

5.56 mm Ameli Machine Gun

Specification

Cartridge: 5.56 x 45 mm NATO

Operating system: Delayed blowback

Weight, empty: 6.35 kg

Length overall: 970 mm

Barrel: 400 mm, 6 grooves, rh

Feed system: 100 or 200-round belt

Rate of Fire: 850 or 1200 rds/min

Muzzle velocity: 875 m/sec

Manufacturer: Santa Barbara SA Madrid, Spain.

Above: The Ameli machine gun loaded with a belt of ammunition. The carrying handle also acts as a lock and handle for removing the barrel, through a slot on the right side of the jacket.

Below: An unusual method of using a light machine gun. Instead of using the bipod, this Spanish soldier is resting the gun on its belt box, which probably allows him to cover a wider arc of fire without having to move his body.

MINIMI 5.56 mm Machine Gun · Belgium

Production of the **Minimi** began in 1982, since which time it has been adopted in many countries, including the USA where it is known as the M249 Squad Automatic Weapon. A conventional gas-actuated gun, it has a simple two-position gas regulator feeding gas from the barrel into a piston which drives the bolt assembly. The bolt carrier moves back and a cam rotates the bolt to unlock it from the breech extension.

Feed is unusual; without any need for adjustment the weapon can fire from a free-hanging belt; from a belt carried in a 200-round belt box clipped to the gun; or from any box magazine using the NATO-standard M16 interface - which includes the British SA80, French FAMAS-G2, Belgian FNC and several others.

The two feed apertures have a simple cover which blocks one feedway when the other is in use, and the bolt assembly has two feed horns so that it can feed from either position.

There are three models of **Minimi**; the standard version is that for which data is given; the lighter and shorter 'Para' version has a telescoping butt and a 347 mm barrel, giving an overall length of 893 mm with the butt extended or 736 with it folded. The weight is 7.1 kg unloaded. The less common vehicle model is simply the standard model but with a closing plate and spade grips on the rear of the receiver instead of a butt-stock.

All models are normally rifled with one turn in 7 inches, so as to perform best with the NATO - standard SS109 cartridge, but they are available rifled one turn in 12 inches to suit the older US M193 pattern ammunition.

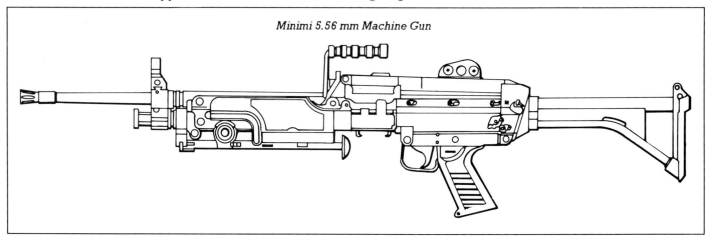

Minimi 5.56 mm Machine Gun

Specification

Cartridge: 5.56 x 45 mm NATO

Operating system: Gas

Weight, empty: 6.83 kg

Length overall: 1040 mm

Barrel: 466 mm, 6 grooves, rh

Feed system: Disintegrating link belt or M16 - type box magazine

Rate of Fire: 700 to 1000 rounds/minute according to feed

Muzzle velocity: 915 m/sec(NATO); 965 m/sec (M193)

Manufacturer: FN Herstal SA, Liege, Belgium.

Below: *The Minimi machine gun in belt-fed mode. Inserting a belt automatically blocks the magazine aperture, so that there is no risk of accidentally jamming the gun by attempting to double feed.*

ULTIMAX 100 5.56 mm Machine Gun   Singapore

Development of the **Ultimax** began in Singapore in 1978 and it was issued to the Singapore armed forces from 1983 onward. It was also evaluated by several other armies, and received favourable reports, but it was unfortunate in that it appeared shortly after the FN Minimi, and several forces which might have considered the Ultimax for adoption were already committed to the Minimi.

The **Ultimax** is an excellent design and deserved wider use. Its principal feature is the exceptionally low recoil force, which allows the gun to be fired at full-automatic, from the hip, using only one hand, something which can be done with very few automatic weapons. This is due to the very long travel of the bolt and the careful design of the return spring system so that the bolt comes to a stop without striking the backplate of the receiver. Much of the recoil force is thus absorbed and there is no violent blow to rotate the gun about its rear end and thus cause it to climb during firing.

Operation is by a gas cylinder above the barrel, in which a piston is driven backwards. This carries the bolt and rotates it to unlock by the usual cam arrangement. The gas piston is hollow and acts as a casing for the very long return spring, which is anchored to the rear of the receiver. On the return stroke of the piston the bolt picks up a round from the magazine and loads it into the chamber, the bolt is rotated to lock and the piston then strikes the firing pin to fire the cartridge. The barrel is somewhat longer than might be expected in a light machine gun and thus the muzzle velocity is high and the accuracy very good.

The '100' part of the title comes from its unique 100-round drum magazine, a genuine magazine and not a belt box, the rounds being fed by spring pressure into the breech. Alternatively, standard 20 or 30 - round rifle magazines can be used.

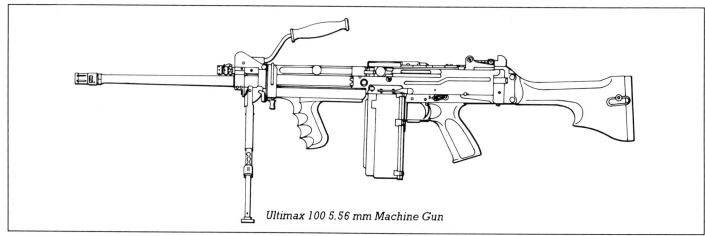

Ultimax 100 5.56 mm Machine Gun

Specification

Cartridge: 5.56 x 45 mm NATO

Operating system: Gas, rotating bolt

Weight, empty: 4.9 kg with bipod

Length overall: 1024 mm

Barrel: 508 mm, 6 grooves, rh

Feed system: 100-round drum, or 20 or 30-round box magazines

Rate of Fire: 600 rounds/min

Muzzle velocity: 970 m/sec

Manufacturer: Chartered Industries of Singapore

Above Right: The Ultimax 100 machine gun fitted with a fixed barrel, the carrying handle being at the centre of gravity.
Centre Right: The Ultimax 100 fitted with the more usual quick-change barrel. The carrying handle on the barrel facilitates changing.
Below Right: The Ultimax 100 with the butt and bolt carrier assembly removed. Note the length of the carrier assembly, which is one of the factors responsible for the relatively soft recoil in this weapon.

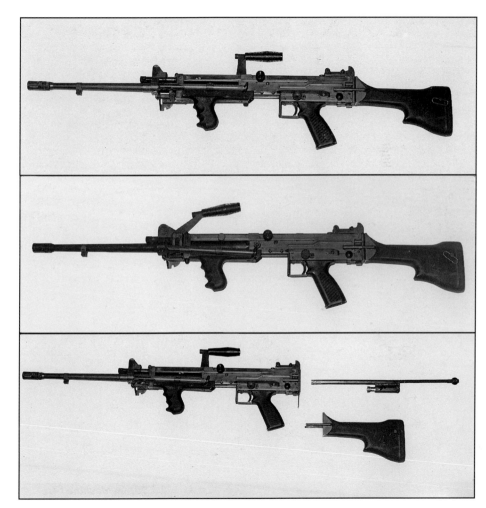

Negev 5.56 mm Light Machine Gun — Israel

The **Negev** is a very versatile weapon which can fire from belts, rifle magazines or drum magazines, can be fired from a bipod or tripod or even from the hip, and can be fitted with barrels of different lengths and with different rifling so as to extract the best performance from either the NATO or American M193 cartridge. With a long barrel it becomes a sustained-fire machine gun; with a short barrel and with the bipod removed, it can be used as an assault rifle. It is the closest anyone has yet come to the truly universal small arm, and it will be interesting to see how the Israeli Army develops it.

It is gas operated, with the usual type of gas piston assembly beneath the barrel. The gas regulator, between barrel and gas cylinder, is adjustable and has three positions. As is usual, the regulator allows more gas to be blown into the system to overcome friction from fouling and dirt, or cut off completely to allow a rifle grenade to be fired from the muzzle. But it also allows a degree of control over the rate of fire; if the gun is clean and correctly lubricated the first position on the regulator allows firing at 650 to 800 rounds per minute; the second position steps this up to 800-950 rounds/min.

By removing the standard 460 mm barrel and replacing it with a 330 mm barrel, and inserting a rifle magazine into the receiver, the **Negev** can be used as an assault rifle. Both barrels are normally rifled one turn in 7 inches, the optimum for the NATO standard 5.56 mm cartridge, but barrels rifled one turn in 12 inches, to suit the lighter American M193 bullet, are available. The regulation magazine is that of the Galil rifle, but M16 magazines (also NATO-standard) can be used with an adapter.

The sights are adjustable up to 1000 metres and have night markers with tritium illumination. In addition most types of military optical and electro-optical sights can be fitted.

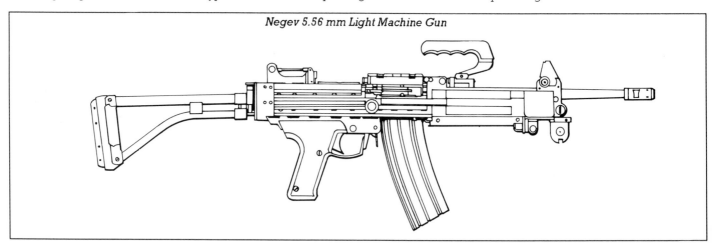

Negev 5.56 mm Light Machine Gun

Specification

Cartridge: 5.56 x 45 mm NATO (or M193)

Operating system: Gas, open bolt, selective fire

Weight, empty: 7.2 kg

Length overall: 1020 mm (long barrel, Stock extended)

Barrel: 460 mm long, 330 mm short; 6 grooves rh
Feed system: Belt, drum or box magazine

Rate of Fire: 650 to 950 rounds/min

Muzzle velocity: c 850 to 1000 m/sec depending on length of barrel and type of ammunition in use.

Manufacturer: Ta'as Israel Industries, Israel.

Above Right: *Negev 7.62 mm Assault rifle with bipod and carrying handle.*
Below Right: *General view of Negev, belt-fed from pouch.*

17

MAG 7.62 mm Machine Gun Belgium

The **FN MAG** (Mitrailleuse a Gaz) was the first post-war General Purpose Machine Gun (GPMG) to appear, and it was adopted into British service as the L7 GPMG as well as being purchased by over 75 other countries. Over 150,000 have been made since its introduction in 1958, most in 7.62 mm calibre but some in 6.5 mm calibre for the Swedish Army.

The **MAG** uses a gas piston to operate the breech block and feed mechanism. The gas piston extends behind the breech block and is connected to the rear of the block by a hinged link. The block moves in guides and is drawn to the rear by a cocking handle. On pressing the trigger the block and piston go forward, pushing a cartridge from the belt into the breech. The nose of the block is guided down to close the breech, and the hinged link at the rear causes the rear end to be forced down in front of lugs in the receiver, so locking it closed. On firing, gas pressure drives the piston back and the link lifts the bolt from the lugs and withdraws it, extracting and ejecting the spent case. A spring is compressed and then drives the breech block and piston forward once more to begin the next firing cycle.

The barrel can be quickly changed when it becomes hot, and there is no need to remove the ammunition belt to do so.

Normally provided with a bipod, the MAG can also be fitted to a tripod for sustained fire in the battalion supporting role, and this gives rise to the 'General Purpose' title. There is also a co-axial version for fitting into tank turrets, and a slightly modified version which can be pod-mounted on helicopters.

A gas regulator at the front of the gas cylinder can be adjusted to admit more gas so as to overcome dirt or fouling after long firing, or it can be used to regulate the rate of fire. Feed is normally from a disintegrating link belt, but the gun can be modified to use continuously articulated belts, though the two types cannot be interchanged without altering the gun.

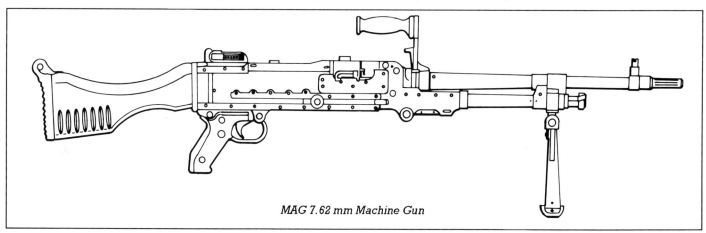

MAG 7.62 mm Machine Gun

Specification

Cartridge: 7.62 x 51 mm NATO

Operating system: Gas

Weight, empty: 11.65 kg

Length overall: 1260 mm

Barrel: 548 mm, 4 grooves, rh

Feed system: disintegrating link belt

Rate of Fire: 650 to 1000 rounds/min

Muzzle velocity: 840 m/sec

Manufacturer: FN Herstal SA, Liege, Belgium.

Above Right: *The essential components of the FN MAG machine gun: upper; the gun with heavy barrel for sustained fire from a tripod; lower; the light barrel with carrying handle and butt.*

Below Right: *The FN MAG in standard form with a bipod. The carrying handle also removes the hot barrel.*

M60 7.62 mm Machine Gun USA

The **M60** appeared in 1957 to accompany the M14 rifle, both weapons introducing the 7.62 mm NATO cartridge to American service. The original version was prone to a number of troubles; it used a feed system taken from the German M42 machine gun which proved too complicated and was redesigned, and the bipod was attached to the barrel, so that changing the barrel meant that the gunner had to support the hot gun while his assistant struggled with a hot barrel. It had a fixed foresight and zero-adjustable backsight, which meant that the gunner had to remember what zero to apply to which barrel; in practice he ignored it and accepted the inaccuracy.

All these problems were ironed out in due course and the **M60** has become a reliable and well-liked weapon. It uses a non-adjustable gas action; once the piston has received sufficient gas pressure to move backwards, it automatically cuts off the gas flow, and the stiffer the action, the more gas it allows before cut-off, so becoming a self-regulating system. A post on the rear end of the gas piston engages in a curved slot in the bolt and so rotates the bolt to unlock it and drive it back, on the return stroke it rotates the bolt and the post then strikes the firing pin to fire the round.

There are now several versions of the **M60**: the **M60C** is a remotely-fired model for mounting on helicopters; the **M60D** is for mounting on helicopters, boats or vehicles and has a spade grip and trigger unit instead of the usual butt; the **M60E2** is for mounting in armoured vehicles; the **M60E3** is a lightweight model with a forward hand grip and a shorter (560 mm) barrel. Zero adjustment is done on the foresight so that each barrel can be accurately zeroed. The **M60E4**, entering service in 1995, is an improved E3 model with stronger bipod, improved belt feed mechanism, a rail mount for optical or electro-optical sights, and the attachment of the trigger unit and pistol grip is improved so that there is less chance of it dropping off during firing. There are also vehicle and co-axial versions of this new model.

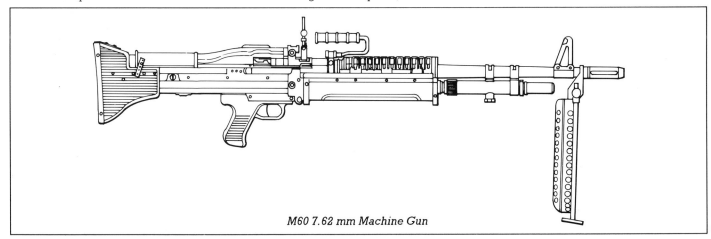

M60 7.62 mm Machine Gun

Specification

Cartridge: 7.62 x 51 mm NATO

Operating system: Gas

Weight, empty: 11.1 kg

Length overall: 1105 mm

Barrel: 560 mm, 6 grooves, rh

Feed system: Disintegrating link belt

Rate of Fire: 600-650 rounds/min

Muzzle velocity: 853 m/sec

Manufacturer: Saco Defense, Saco, Maine.

Above Right: *The lightweight M60 machine Gun, which has now been perfected into the M60E4, features a forward grip which gives the gunner better control and permits firing on the move.*

Below Right: *The M60 in its original form, here being fired by a British soldier visiting the US army. Note that the bipod is attached to the barrel, which raised problems when changing a hot barrel.*

MG3 7.62 mm Machine Gun   Germany

When the German Army was reconstituted in the 1950s they required a General Purpose Machine Gun, and after studying what was available decided that none of them were as good as the **MG42** they had used during the war. They therefore put it back into production in 1959 in 7.62 mm NATO calibre, calling it the **MG1**. This weapon used a continuous-link belt. At the same time a number of wartime **MG42** were converted to 7.62 mm calibre and became the **MG2**. The German belt was not standardised within NATO and therefore the gun was slightly re-designed in 1968 to use either the German belt or the NATO-standard disintegrating link belt. This became the **MG3** and has remained in service ever since. It is also manufactured under licence in Greece, Italy, Pakistan, Spain and Turkey.

The Yugoslavian Army also use a copy of the original **MG42** in 7.92 mm calibre.

The **MG3** uses a roller-locked breech very similar to that used in the Ameli machine gun, but in this case the rollers lock into an extension of the barrel, and when the gun fires both barrel and bolt recoil locked together. After a short movement, during which the bullet leaves the barrel and the breech pressure drops, the rollers are forced in by cams in the receiver, so unlocking the bolt from the barrel and allowing it to run back, extracting and ejecting the empty case, and then return to feed and fire the next round.

The barrel is held in a perforated cooling jacket which is slotted on the right side. The barrel has a locking handle at the right rear, and changing barrels is simply

a matter of pushing this handle forward to unlock and release the barrel from the receiver, and then pulling the barrel backwards and sideways out of the slot. The new barrel is slipped in and locked in place and the gun is ready to fire in seconds. Frequent barrel changes are necessary due to the high rate of fire.

The **MG3** is fitted with a bipod for use as the squad light machine gun; it can also be tripod-mounted for continuous fire roles and a variety of indirect-fire and optical and electro-optical sights are available. A recent adoption has been a belt drum which holds about 150 rounds and can be clipped to the bottom of the gun rather like a drum magazine. This avoids having lengths of belt dangling from the gun and attracting dirt during tactical moves.

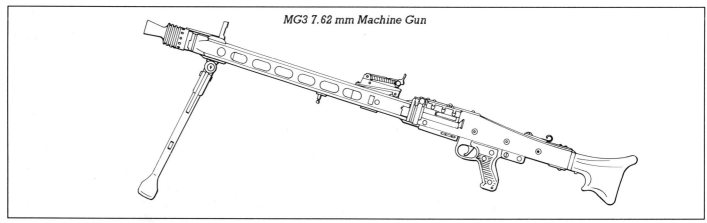

MG3 7.62 mm Machine Gun

Specification

Cartridge: 7.62 x 51 mm NATO

Operating system: Recoil, roller locked

Weight, empty: 11.05 kg with bipod

Length overall: 1225 mm

Barrel: 531 mm, 6 grooves, rh

Feed system: Disintegrating link belt

Rate of Fire: 1100 rounds/min

Muzzle velocity: 820 m/sec

Manufacturer: Rheinmetall GmbH,
                Dusseldorf

Above Right: *Firing the MG3 from the hip. The weight is supported by the sling, and the soldier uses his left hand to keep the barrel down against its tendency to rise during automatic fire.*

Below Right: *A soldier of the Bundeswehr firing the MG3 from a bipod in the squad support role.*

PK 7.62 mm Machine Gun Family   F. Soviet Union

This machine gun appeared in Soviet service in the early 1960s and has since been modified and adapted until a complete family of guns replaced a number of individual guns. The design is by Kalashnikov, and is an amalgamation of ideas from several other weapons. The rotating bolt is the same as that of the AK47 rifle, the barrel change is adapted from the earlier SG42 machine gun, the feed system driven by the gas piston comes from a Czech design, and the trigger mechanism is from the earlier Degtyarev DP machine gun. What is most remarkable is that the weapon has been designed around the old 7.62 mm rimmed cartridge which has been in service since 1891.

A rimmed cartridge does nothing to make the feed system easy, but Kalashnikov appears to have got round all the problems and has produced a reliable and efficient weapon. The advantage is, that this old full-power cartridge can produce lethal results out to a much greater range than the standard 7.62 x 39 mm rimless rifle cartridge.

The family consists of the **PK**, the basic gun, with a heavy fluted barrel and weighing about 9 kg. The **PKS** is this basic gun mounted on a tripod which can be adjusted for either ground fire or anti-aircraft fire. The **PKT** is designed for co-axial mounting in armoured vehicle turrets; it has the sights, trigger unit and stock removed and a longer and heavier barrel and an electrical solenoid firing mechanism installed.

The **PKM** is a 'product-improved' **PK**, with a lighter barrel and overall construction to bring the weight down to about 8.4 kg. It is easily recognised by its cut-out butt and the 100-round belt-box slung beneath the receiver. The **PKMS** is the **PKM** mounted on a tripod. The **PKM** became the company support weapon for the Warsaw Pact armies, while the **PKS** version was the sustained-fire support weapon. The widespread adoption of these weapons led to their manufacture in Romania and Bulgaria and they were also copied in China as the 'Type 80'

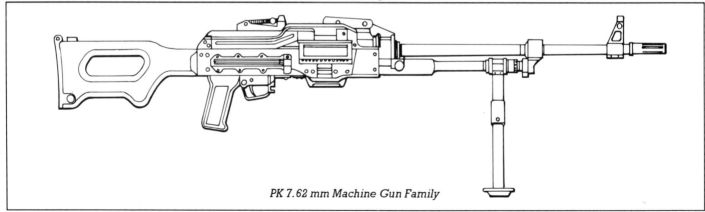

PK 7.62 mm Machine Gun Family

Specifications:

Cartridge: 7.62 x 54R Mosin-Nagant

Operating system: Gas, rotating bolt

Weight, empty: 9.0 kg

Length overall: 1160 mm

Barrel: 658 mm, 4 grooves, rh

Feed system: 100, 200 or 250-round belt

Rate of Fire: 700 rounds/min

Muzzle velocity: 825 m/sec

Manufacturer: State Arsenals

Above Right: *The PKM machine gun in its light support role, complete with the 100-round belt box.*

Below Right: *Another PKM machine gun; the original PM model had a fluted barrel to provide extra cooling area, a refinement found unnecessary on the PKM which has a smooth barrel.*

BROWNING .50 in. M2HB Machine Gun   USA

The basic mechanism of this gun first appeared during World War One as the **.30 Browning M1917** machine gun. After the war the design was enlarged to fire a new .50 calibre cartridge and became the **.50 M1921**, principally used as an anti-aircraft weapon. In the 1930s the US Cavalry demanded a heavy air cooled gun for use on vehicles, and the **M2HB** (Heavy Barrel) was the result, being adopted for service in 1933. Since then it has been built by the hundreds of thousands and is in use all over the world.

The **M2HB** is recoil operated. On firing, barrel and breech-block recoil together for about 18 mm, after which the breech lock,

a vertical plate sliding up in a barrel extension and engaging in the underside of the bolt, is driven down to unlock the bolt. The barrel now stops and the block continues rearward against a spring, stops, and goes forward again to collect a cartridge from the feedway and load it into the chamber. The barrel moves forward, the breech lock slides upwards and as the barrel and breech-block come to rest, securely locked together, the firing pin goes forward to fire the cartridge. One slight drawback to the **M2HB** was that the barrel is screwed into the barrel extension, and its positioning is critical in order to give the correct clearance for the cartridge headspace. In the 1970s

FN of Belgium, the principal licensees of the Browning design, developed a Quick-Change Barrel (QCB) system which allows a rapid change without the need for critical adjustment. Similar systems have since been developed by other manufacturers such as Saco and Ramo in the USA and Manroy in Britain.

Another complaint was of the weight of the gun; this was remedied by the development of a lightweight version by Ramo in the USA. This has 75 % common parts with the standard gun, but the receiver is of high-strength lightweight material and the shorter (914 mm) barrel reduces the weight to 26.7 kg.

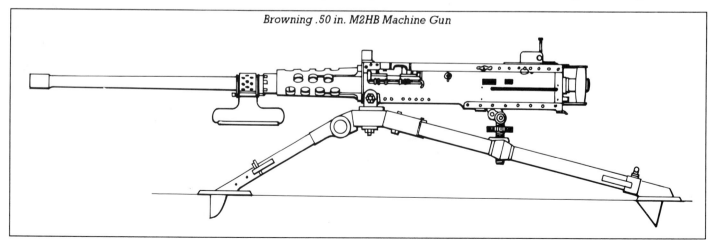

Browning .50 in. M2HB Machine Gun

Specification

Cartridge: .50 Browning (12.7 x 99 mm)

Operating system: Short recoil

Weight, empty: 38.15 kg

Length overall: 1656 mm

Barrel: 1143 mm, 8 grooves, rh

Feed system: Disintegrating link belt

Rate of Fire: 485 to 635 rounds/min

Muzzle velocity: 916 m/sec

Manufacturers: Various

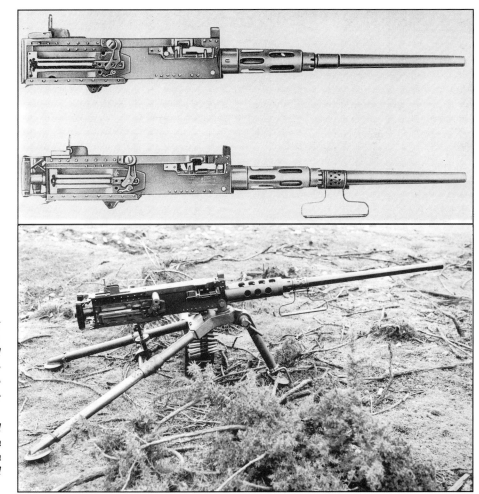

Above Right: *Two versions of the Browning M2HB machine gun. Upper, the 'fixed' gun for installation in aircraft and armoured vehicles. Lower, the flexible gun for use on tripods or by aerial gunners, with spade grips for control and a handle on the barrel for changing purposes.*

Below Right: *The M2HB on a ground tripod in the heavy infantry support role. It is often seen with more complex tripods which unfold so as to allow the gun to be used in the air defence role.*

JACKHAMMER Combat Shotgun

USA

In the early 1980s the US forces were looking for a purpose-built combat shotgun to replace the various commercial shotguns which had been put to use in the past. One of the responses to this programme was the **Jackhammer**; however, by the time the **Jackhammer** and other contenders were ready the combat shotgun programme had been sacrificed to budget cuts, and military adoption never happened. The makers of the **Jackhammer** continued with their development and now have the Mk3-A2 ready for production. Several military and security forces have expressed interest.

The **Jackhammer** is a 12-gauge shotgun firing commercial 12-ga 70 mm cartridges from a revolving cylinder which in this case is known as the 'Ammo Cassette'. It is not part of the weapon, being a plastic moulding which is supplied fully loaded with the ammunition of choice and shrink-wrapped. This can be slipped into place on the weapon in a second or two and the weapon is then cocked by sliding the fore-end back like a pump gun. On pressing the trigger the shot cartridge aligned with the barrel is fired and the gas pressure causes the barrel to move forward as the shot exits. This unlocks the barrel from the cylinder and an operating rod attached to the barrel, working in cam grooves in the cylinder, rotates the cylinder one-tenth of a turn to index the next round into place.

The barrel then runs back, driven by a spring, to re-engage with the cylinder, so making a gas-tight joint between cylinder and barrel. The movement of the operating rod also cocks the firing mechanism; there is a de-cocking lever inside the buttstock aperture which allows the weapon to be safely de-cocked if not required to shoot.

When the Ammo Cassette has been emptied, a simple movement of the fore-end allows it to drop out, to be replaced by a fresh, loaded cassette. It is also possible to take a loaded cassette, fit a special pressure plate to it, and bury it in the ground as an anti-personnel mine which discharges 12 shotgun cartridges upwards when disturbed.

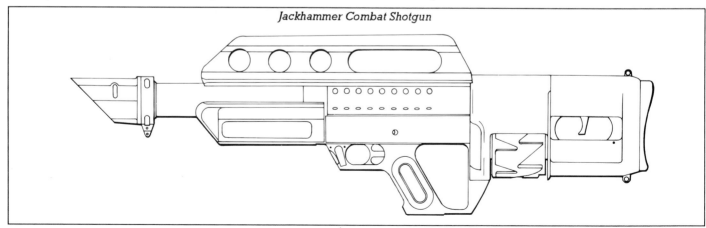

Jackhammer Combat Shotgun

Specification

Cartridge: 12-bore 70 mm shotgun

Operating system: Gas

Weight, empty: 4.57 kg

Length overall: 787 mm

Barrel: 525 mm

Feed system: 10-shot rotating cylinder

Rate of Fire: 240 rounds/min

Manufacturer: Mark Three Corporation

Above: *The Jackhammer Mk3-A2 combat shotgun ready for firing with its 'Ammo Cassette' in place.*

Below: *The Jackhammer with the 'Ammo Cassette' removed and with a second cassette prepared for use as a 'Bear Trap' anti-personnel mine.*

Weapon Sights

Most weapons are provided with "iron-sights", normally an adjustable aperture backsight and a fixed blade foresight, which is adequate for short-range firing. But the use of an optical sight makes aiming easier, especially in poor light, and more and more military rifles are being provided with low-power optical sights. When night descends, more complex sights are required. The **Image Intensifying (I-I) Sight** takes whatever light there is - starlight or moonlight - and amplifies the contrast some 20, 000 times so that a recognisable picture can be seen and targets up to 300 metres or more can be easily engaged. Early models, the "first generation", were heavy and required three stages of amplification to get a reasonable picture; newer models - the second and third generations - feature improved technology and only one stage of amplification is required so that the sight becomes lighter and more compact.

Image intensifying sights only work when there is light to intensify. When there is no light whatever they are useless. Because of this, much work has been put into infra-red or **Thermal Imaging (TI) Sights** which can see in total darkness. These first appeared in World War II but were cumbersome, unreliable and and noisy. Today's TI sights are still rather large but silent and long

ranging, and they deliver a picture almost as informative as a television screen. They also have the ability, since they rely on detecting heat rather than light, of being able to "see" the heat source behind a bush or behind a camouflage net, something no optical sight can do. And since, unlike an I-I sight, they can be used in day light, they have become valuable tools for searching out concealed targets invisible to the naked eye or binoculars.

Below: CLASS - Computerised Laser Sight System - consists of a laser range finder, and electro-optical day and night telescope and a ballistic computer. Fed with the ballistics of the weapon the target range and speed, and the meteorological conditions, CLASS calculates the precise trajectory and adjusts the sight so that all the gunner has to do is put the crosswires on the target and pull the trigger. It is currently going into service with the Canadian Army for crew-served weapons.

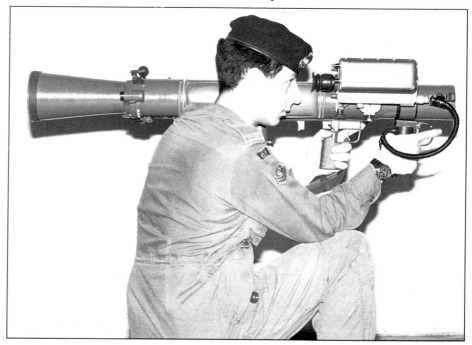

Above: *A typical mortar sight, this being a Swiss design: the upper section revolves, and scales indicate the direction, while the lower section contains a level bubble which is displaced when the range is set and brought level again by elevating or depressing the barrel.*

Above Right: *A typical Thermal Imaging (infra-red) weapon sight. Still somewhat bulky and heavier than a second-generation I-I sight, in total darkness it is the only option.*

Below Right: *In comparison, a typical second-generation I-I sight, the French Sopelem OB50, mounted on the American M16 rifle. The performance is better than that of the first-generation sight and the size and weight less than half.*

FLY-K Weapon System

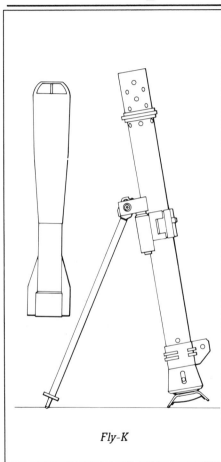

Fly-K

This unusual weapon was originally developed in Belgium in the early 1980s, but the company failed and the design was purchased by a French company which continued the development. The weapon is now in use by the French Marines and sales to other countries have also been made.

The **Fly-K** is a flashless, smokeless, almost-silent mortar. These characteristics necessarily mean a short range, but as a light and undetectable weapon for use by raiding parties, it is in a class of its own. The effect of mortar bombs descending on your head when you cannot hear anything firing is rather un-nerving.

The mortar itself is simply a lightweight tube within which is a central steel post or spigot, a trigger-operated firing mechanism, and a spade-type baseplate. The bomb is a high explosive warhead with a finned hollow tail unit of high-strength steel, inside which is the propelling cartridge. The bomb is loaded into the mortar tube so that the hollow tail fits over the central spigot. When the trigger is pressed the firing pin snaps forward and fires the cartridge. The explosion shears off the lower end of the cartridge and forces it out against the wall of the tail unit and then downwards against the tip of the spigot. The result is to blow the bomb off the end of the spigot with sufficient force for it to travel up to 675 metres range. Moreover, the cartridge base, pressed tightly against the wall of the tail tube, retains all the propulsive gas inside the tube; the base jams firmly against a specially-formed lip when it reaches the end of the tail tube, so that the bomb flies off carrying the combustion gas, heat and smoke sealed up inside it. There is thus no detectable 'signature'; it cannot be found by flash, smoke or infra-red emissions, and the sound is generally lost in the background noise.

The mortar unit weighs 4 kg, with a simple sight; the bombs weigh 765 grammes and the usual range of high explosive, smoke and illuminating bombs is available. An unusual feature is that because the entire bomb does not enter the barrel of the mortar, the actual warhead portion can be of whatever diameter is found most effective for the payload.

Specification:

Calibre: 51 mm

Elevation: Free to 85°

Traverse: Free

Weight in firing position: 4.80 kg

Maximum range: 675 m

Minimum range: 40 m

Maximum muzzle velocity: 88.5 m/sec

Rate of fire: 25 rounds/min

Manufacturer: Titanite SA France

Near Right: *The PRB Fly-K mortar is easily carried by the soldier.*

Far Right: *The Fly-K in the firing position. Most of the barrel space is occupied by the central firing spigot.*

L9A1 51 mm Mortar

The British army adopted a 2 inch calibre mortar in the 1930s which, during World War Two, proved to be a handy quick support weapon for the infantry platoon, with a maximum range of about 500 metres. After the old 3 inch mortar had been replaced by the 81 mm model, the 2 inch was then improved into this 51 mm version by applying much the same sort of engineering-improving the bomb and making the weapon more accurate.

The barrel is a simple steel tube, bell-mouthed to strengthen the muzzle and make loading easier, and closed at the rear end by a breech-piece which is retained by spring-loaded plungers. Inside this breech-piece is a self-cocking trigger mechanism, and the entire barrel assembly is attached to a rectangular spade. A sight

clamps to the side of the barrel, and a sling is provided for carrying on the soldier's back. To fire, the soldier simply plants the spade on the ground, sets the range on his sight, drops a bomb into the muzzle, raises the mortar until the spirit-bubble on the sight is level, points it in the right direction and then pulls the trigger.

The standard bomb is a 920-gramme high explosive bomb of very modern construction, using a light metal body with an internal wrapping of notched wire to provide the desired fragments. There is also a smoke bomb capable of providing a useful concealing screen, and an illuminating bomb which carries a parachute and flare capable of producing 170,000 candle-power to light up the battlefield; this bomb is particularly useful to silhouette tanks at

night and thus provide a prominent target.

A unique feature of this weapon is the method used to permit accurate firing at very short ranges. Most small mortars simply point the barrel at a very high angle and throw the bomb high into the air to drop somewhat inaccurately at short range. The 51 mm uses a 'short range insert', a steel support with a long central firing pin which is dropped into the barrel. The bomb is then loaded, to rest on top of this insert, and pulling the trigger actuates the long firing pin to fire the bomb. The effect is to allow the expansion of propellant gas into a large space behind the bomb, thus reducing the pressure and velocity and so reducing the range without affecting accuracy.

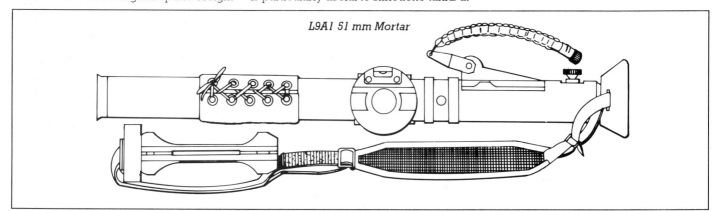

L9A1 51 mm Mortar

Specification

Cartridge: 5.56 x 45 mm NATO

Operating system: Gas

Weight, empty: 6.83 kg

Length overall: 1040 mm

Barrel: 466 mm, 6 grooves, rh

Feed system: Disintegrating link belt or M16 - type box magazine

Rate of Fire: 700 to 1000 rounds/minute according to feed

Muzzle velocity: 915 m/sec (NATO);

965 m/sec (M193)

Manufacturer: FN Herstal SA, Liege, Belgium.

Picture: Firing the British 51mm mortar. The sight can be seen below the mortarman's left hand and the trigger and firing lanyard are just behind it.

HIRTENBERGER 60 mm Commando Mortar Austria

Adopted by the Austrian Army in 1990, this design originated with the Bohler company, who were absorbed by Hirtenberger AG in 1992. Hirtenberger, primarily an ammunition company, had designed and manufactured the ammunition for Bohler and it was a logical move for them to take over the manufacture of the complete system.

Like most lightweight 60 mm weapons, the 'Commando' mortar can be easily carried by one man, either in a specially-designed back-pack or simply slung from his shoulder. The mortar itself consists of a simple tube screwed into a breech-piece which contains the firing pin and which ends in a small circular baseplate. There is also a prominent hand-grip which allows easy carriage for short distances and which also contains the thumb-operated trigger for the firing mechanism.

No bipod or tripod support is provided; instead, a heat-resistant plastic sleeve shrunk around the barrel acts as a hand grip, and elevation is assessed by means of the sling. This is studded with brass marker strips marked with various ranges, and in order to fire at, say 1000 metres, the soldier simply plants the baseplate in the ground and allows the sling to fall to the ground in a loop. He then locates the marker for 1000 metres and puts his foot on the sling at this point. Then he pulls up on the barrel until the sling is tight between the barrel and his foot, and this automatically gives the barrel approximately the correct elevation. He now points the barrel in the right direction, drops a bomb down the barrel, grips the hand-grip and presses on the trigger. This releases the firing pin and the bomb is fired, with sufficient accuracy to drop it in the area of the target, from where the firer can make adjustments to bring the next bomb accurately on to the target. This is the recommended practice when speed is the ruling factor; when more deliberate fire is possible, then a graduated sight can be clipped to the barrel and a more accurate elevation and line can be achieved.

Where the trigger feature is not required, an alternative model is available with a fixed firing pin; this is adequate for most firing, but where low-angle fire is desirable the self-cocking trigger mechanism is preferable.

Hirtenberger 60 mm Commando Mortar

Specification

Calibre: 60 mm

Elevation: Free, to 90°

Traverse: Free

Weight in firing position: 5.10 kg

Maximum range: 2600 m

Minimum range: 60 m

Maximum muzzle velocity: 199 m/sec

Rate of fire: 30 rounds/min

Manufacturer: Hirtenberger AG Austria

An Austrian soldier aiming the Hirtenberger 60 mm Commando mortar, using an accessory 'monopod' support strut, useful when the firer wishes to lie prone and avoid attracting attention.

ECIA 60 mm Commando Mortar — Spain

This is one of the lightest and simplest mortars in service with any army, yet has a respectable range and fires the same 2.05 kg streamlined bomb as the standard 60 mm mortar. It is in service with the Spanish Army and has been exported to several other countries.

The 'Commando' consists of a short steel barrel with a small circular baseplate at the lower end. There is a canvas sleeve around the barrel, which the soldier holds while firing, and attached to this is a sling by which he can carry it.

A simple sight is clipped to the barrel by a hose clip. This has a bar with foresight and backsight, pivoted in its centre and moving across a circular scale of ranges. The centre of the bar carries a simple bubble level. The soldier simply turns the bar to the correct range, then grasps the mortar by the canvas sleeve and, placing the baseplate firmly on the ground, raises the muzzle until the bubble is centralised in its housing. He then uses the sight to point the mortar in the right direction, and with his other hand places a bomb into the muzzle and allows it to drop down to strike the firing pin. He then observes where the bomb goes and, by either adjusting the sight or, more probably, by estimation based on experience, raises or lowers the barrel and adjusts the direction and fires another round. In this way he corrects the fall of shot onto his target and then fires for effect.

In addition to the high explosive bomb the mortar is able to fire the full range of 60 mm bombs, which includes white phosphorous smoke and an illuminating bomb which is particularly useful for firing behind a target so as to silhouette it for engagement by other types of weapon at night.

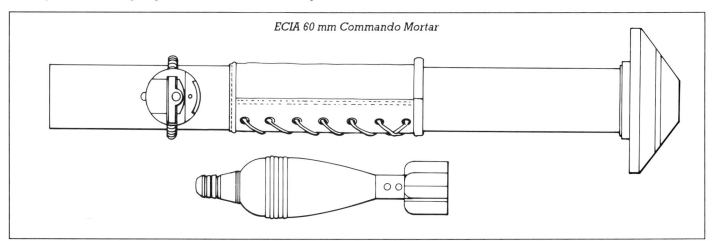

ECIA 60 mm Commando Mortar

Specification

Calibre: 60 mm

Elevation: Free to 90°

Traverse: Free

Weight in firing position: 6.5 kg

Maximum range: 1290 m

Minimum range: 50 m

Rate of fire: 15 rounds/min

Manufacturer: Esperanza y Cia, Spain

Firing the ECIA Commando mortar. This experienced Spanish mortarman has not bothered to fit the sight, relying on his own skill and estimation to judge the angle of the elevation and the direction.

ECIA 60 mm Model L Mortar

Spain

Esperanza & Co have been making mortars since the 1920s; their products equip the Spanish and several other armies, and the British 2 inch mortar of World War 2 came from their drawing board. The 60 mm **Model L** is a good example of their design and of the heavier type of platoon support mortar.

Light enough to be carried by one man, the **Model L** is a 'complete' mortar, with barrel, supporting tripod, baseplate and optical sight. The steel barrel is threaded to take a breech cap which contains a selective firing mechanism; this allows instantaneous drop-firing or trigger firing as preferred; a safety switch withdraws the firing pin from the barrel and completely prevents firing. The cap ends in a ball fitting into a socket on the circular baseplate, allowing the barrel to be swung in any direction. The simple tripod attaches to the barrel by a collar and has a screw elevating system.

The standard projectile is the Model AE bomb, introduced in 1984 and incorporating all the most modern technology; it is highly streamlined and is fitted with a plastic sealing ring around the waist which permits drop firing but seals the propellant gases behind it for maximum efficiency. The high explosive bomb weighs 2.05 kg and has a forged aluminium tail fin unit into which the primary cartridge fits and around which the five secondary cartridges are clipped. Two smoke bombs, one using white phosphorus and the other a pyrotechnic smoke composition, are available to suit individual preferences, and an illuminating bomb can produce 250,000 candle-power for 25 seconds to illuminate a large area.

Where a greater range is desirable, the **Model LL** mortar can be used. This is similar to the **Model L** but the barrel is heavier and stronger so as to allow firing an extra secondary charge to produce a maximum range of 4800 metres with the same bombs. The **Model LL** also differs in being drop-fired only, without the option of firing by means of a trigger. The only drawback is that the entire mortar now weighs just under 18 kg, though this is still within the carrying power of a single man. Special back-packs are provided to which the various pieces of the mortar can be strapped to allow carrying in the most comfortable mode.

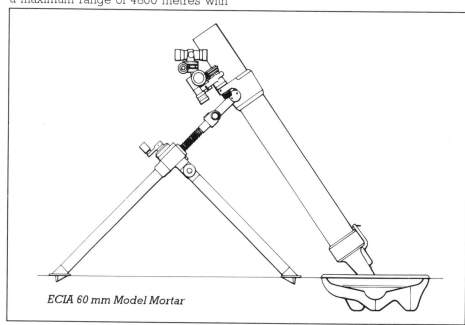

ECIA 60 mm Model Mortar

Specification

Calibre: 60 mm

Elevation: 45° to 80°

Traverse: 8° right and left

Weight in firing position: 12.0 kg

Maximum range: 3800 m

Rate of fire: 30 rounds/min

Manufacturer: Esperanza y Compania

Near Right Upper: *The ECIA 60 mm Model L mortar in the firing position, showing the three basic parts - barrel, tripod and baseplate - of all mortars.*

Near Right Lower: *Transporting the ECIA Model L mortar by using a specially designed pack frame which holds the three components securely.*

Far Right: *The standard 60 mm Type N bombs used with the model L mortar, high explosive, practice and smoke.*

BREDA 81 mm Mortar   Italy

Other things being equal, lengthening the barrel of any firearm will increase the performance because it allows more time for the expanding explosive gases to act upon the projectile to accelerate it, so increasing velocity and range. This principle is more applicable to mortars, because of the fast-burning propellant powders used, and has been applied by the Italian company of Breda in this instance so as to achieve a long range mortar without going to the expense of special and more powerful ammunition.

The barrel of the **Breda** mortar is 1455 mm long, developed at a time when the average length was about 1100 mm. The improved gas efficiency gives this weapon a maximum range of 5000 metres with a 4.2 kg bomb, and yet the whole mortar is light enough to be dismantled and carried by three men. Another useful feature is the ability to withdraw the firing pin completely from the breech-piece, so making the mortar incapable of firing accidentally when a misfired bomb has to be removed.

The standard projectile is the 4.2 kg conventional high explosive bomb, but the **Breda** mortar has a most impressive range of highly advanced bombs available to it. These include the usual white phosphorous smoke bomb and illuminating bomb, and in addition a base ejection smoke bomb which ejects burning smoke candles in mid-air. These fall to the ground to deliver a clinging smoke screen with a longer duration than the white phosphorous bomb. Most novel is the 'sub-munition' bomb made by the SNIA company; this carries nine 'bomblets' inside the main bomb body. A time fuze on the main bomb blows off the nose at a point above the target and the bomblets are thrown clear, falling on to the target below. Each bomblet carries a small shaped explosive charge and an impact fuze and is capable of penetrating up to 60 mm of armour plate, which is quite sufficient to damage any armoured personnel carrier and even penetrate the engine covers of heavy tanks. A similar bomb, the S6, is made by the Simmel company; this also holds nine bomblets which have the same anti-armour performance.

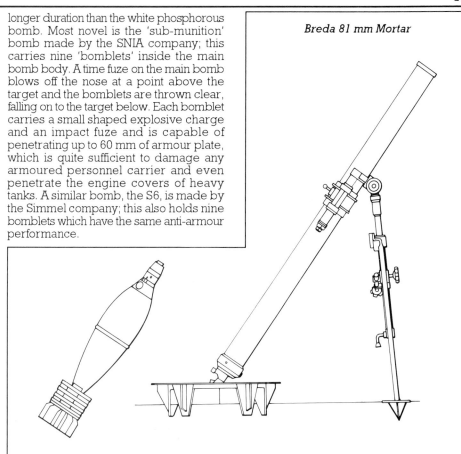

Breda 81 mm Mortar

Specification

Calibre: 81 mm

Elevation: 35° to 85°

Traverse: 8° right and left

Weight in firing position: 43.0 kg

Maximum range: 5000 m

Minimum range: 75 m

Maximum muzzle velocity: 275 m/sec

Rate of fire: 20 rounds/min

Manufacturer: Breda Maccanica
                Bresciana, Italy

Italian marines with their Breda 81 mm mortar.

M3 81 mm Mortar

South Africa

When South Africa became independent, it acquired modern mortars from the Hotchkiss-Brandt company of France. By the time that these were due for replacement a general embargo on the supply of arms to South Africa was in force and the country therefore had to develop its own arms industry, which it did to very good effect. So far as mortars were concerned, the simplest course was to take the existing French design and reproduce it, with a few minor changes, which would better suit the local manufacturing methods. And therefore the South African M3 is essentially the same as the Hotchkiss-Brandt MO-81-61.

The M3 is a conventional three-piece equipment-barrel, baseplate and bipod - with a fixed firing pin to permit drop-firing only. The bipod is attached to the barrel by a collar with a hydraulic shock-absorbing joint. The sight is supported on the bipod, so that the firing shock is dissipated by the shock joint and does not disturb the sight unduly. The bipod has a central elevating screw, and one leg is screw-adjustable for cross-levelling the mortar. The top of the elevating screw carries a traversing arrangement which allows sufficient movement for the engagement of targets and adjustment of fire; where bigger movement is required, the bipod is lifted, moved and repositioned.

The sight is a modern design, developed in South Africa, and uses 'Betalight' tritium light sources for night firing.

The standard bomb is a streamlined steel design using a central plastic sealing ring to give increased efficiency and accuracy. The high explosive bomb weighs 4.4 kg, is loaded with RDX/TNT, carries seven secondary cartridges and is fitted with an impact and delay fuze which is also based on a French design. The smoke bomb is similar in design but filled with titanium tetrachloride and a small explosive charge. On impact the charge breaks open the bomb and scatters the chemical which reacts with the water vapour in the air to develop a dense white smoke for screening purposes. The titanium compound is used in preference to the more common white phosphorus since it carries much less incendiary risk, a factor of some importance in the dry South African bush country.

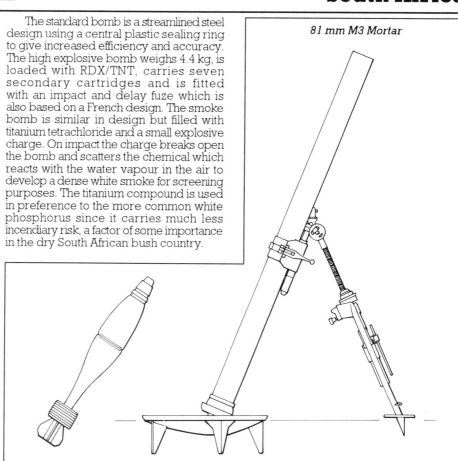

81 mm M3 Mortar

Specification:

Calibre: 81 mm

Elevation: 45° to 90°

Traverse: 15° right and left

Weight in firing position: 42.8 kg

Maximum range: 5000 m

Minimum range: 100 m

Maximum muzzle velocity: 279 m/sec

Rate of fire: 15 rounds/min

Manufacturer: Denel Pty, South Africa

South African troops firing the 81 mm M3 mortar. The layer holds the muzzle cover to allow the loader to place the bomb in the muzzle, while the third member of the team holds the next bomb ready to pass it to the loader.

L16 81 mm Mortar UK

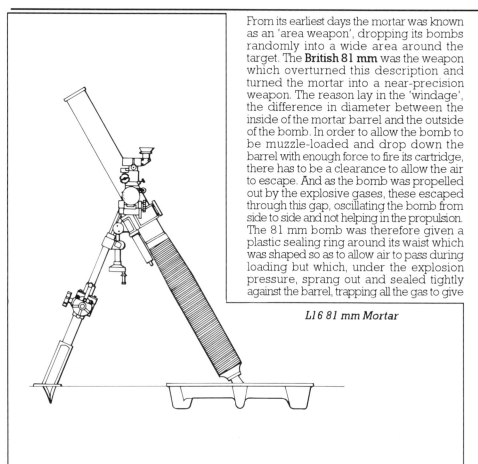

L16 81 mm Mortar

From its earliest days the mortar was known as an 'area weapon', dropping its bombs randomly into a wide area around the target. The **British 81 mm** was the weapon which overturned this description and turned the mortar into a near-precision weapon. The reason lay in the 'windage', the difference in diameter between the inside of the mortar barrel and the outside of the bomb. In order to allow the bomb to be muzzle-loaded and drop down the barrel with enough force to fire its cartridge, there has to be a clearance to allow the air to escape. And as the bomb was propelled out by the explosive gases, these escaped through this gap, oscillating the bomb from side to side and not helping in the propulsion. The 81 mm bomb was therefore given a plastic sealing ring around its waist which was shaped so as to allow air to pass during loading but which, under the explosion pressure, sprang out and sealed tightly against the barrel, trapping all the gas to give better velocity and range, and stabilizing the bomb so as to improve the accuracy.

The rear portion of the barrel is finned, to give a greater surface area for heat dissipation, so that it is possible to keep up a steady rate of 15 bombs a minute for long periods without overheating. The bipod, supporting the barrel, is of an unusual 'K' shape which allows the elevating screw to be contained on one leg and thus save weight. The baseplate is circular, of cast aluminium, and allows the barrel to be swung round through the full 360° by simply moving the bipod, allowing rapid alignment against targets in any direction.

A 4.2 kg high explosive bomb is the standard projectile, and a white phosphorous smoke bomb is also provided. A recent addition to the armoury is the 'Merlin' guided anti-tank projectile, a shaped charge bomb with a millimetric wave seeker head which detects tank targets and steers the bomb to impact, giving the mortar an impressive long range anti-armour capability.

A precise optical sight is fitted, and the mortar squad use the 'Morzen' fire control computer, a hand-held device which can rapidly calculate firing data and store data on targets so that they can be rapidly re-engaged when necessary.

As well as being used in the normal ground role, an 81 mm mortar L16 can be mounted in armoured vehicles, firing through a hatch. It has been adopted by the US Army as the Mortar **M252** and by several other armies around the world.

Specification

Calibre: 81 mm

Elevation: 45° to 80°

Traverse: 7° right and left without moving bipod

Weight in firing position: 37.85 kg inc. sight

Maximum Range: 5650 m

Minimum Range: 166 m

Maximum muzzle velocity: 297 m/sec

Rate of fire: 15 rounds/min

Manufacturer: Royal Ordnance UK

British soldiers firing the 81 mm L16 mortar. The loader is holding a high explosive bomb in the muzzle, awaiting the order to fire, when he will release the bomb and duck down below the muzzle to avoid the worst of the blast.

HIRTENBERGER M12-111 120 mm Mortar   Austria

This heavy mortar was developed to meet a requirement by the Austrian Army, and entered Austrian service in 1985. Normally mounted on a two-wheeled trailer for transport, it can also be installed inside armoured personnel carriers.

The barrel is of high-grade electronic slag refined steel, bell-mouthed to facilitate loading and closed at the rear by a screwed breech-piece which contains the firing mechanism. This can be adjusted to fire either in the fixed mode or as a trigger-operated device. There is an external trigger lever to which a lanyard can be attached, and an external safety lever which completely withdraws the firing pin into the breech-piece.

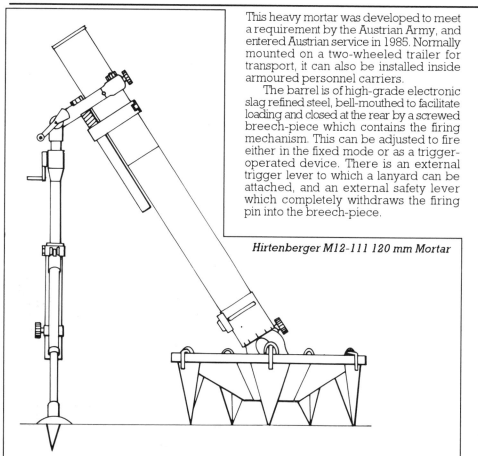

Hirtenberger M12-111 120 mm Mortar

The bipod is symmetrical, with a central elevating screw mechanism on top of which is the traversing screw. The bipod attaches to the barrel by means of a clamp. A dual shock absorber system is interposed, which reduces the recoil blow on both bipod and baseplate.

The baseplate is circular, of steel, and has six radial ribs on the under-surface so as to give a positive grip in any ground conditions. There is a quick-release catch to hold the mortar breech-piece, and lifting hands which also act as locking brackets when the baseplate is fitted to the trailer.

The trailer is a two-wheeled frame on to which the entire mortar can be lowered by a simple winch mechanism; it is not necessary to dismantle the mortar to place it on the trailer, so that it can be brought in or out of action in a few seconds by a trained crew.

Ammunition provided for the 120 mm mortar consists of the usual high explosive, smoke and illuminating bombs. The HE bomb weighs 14.5 kg, has a primary and seven secondary cartridges, and bursts into about 4000 lethal fragments.

When fitted into an armoured vehicle, the mortar uses a slightly shorter barrel and a specially adapted mounting on which the bipod can travel around a track set in the vehicle floor to give about 45° of traverse. A baseplate and standard bipod are also carried in the vehicle so that the mortar can be removed and used as a ground weapon if necessary.

Specification

Calibre: 120 mm

Elevation: 39° to 83°

Traverse: 16.8° on bipod

Weight in firing position: 277 kg

Maximum range: 9000 m

Minimum range: 400 m

Maximum muzzle velocity: 430 m/sec

Rate of fire: 10 rounds/min

Manufacturer: Hirtenberger AG, Austria

Preparing to fire the Hirtenberger M12-111 120 mm mortar. The gunner is setting the sight, while his assistant is preparing the ammunition.

M74 120 mm Light Mortar   Yugoslavia

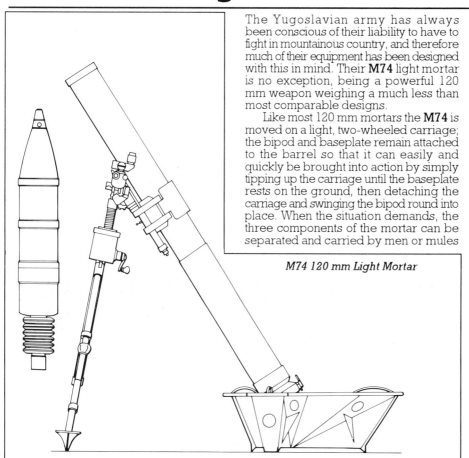

The Yugoslavian army has always been conscious of their liability to have to fight in mountainous country, and therefore much of their equipment has been designed with this in mind. Their **M74** light mortar is no exception, being a powerful 120 mm weapon weighing a much less than most comparable designs.

Like most 120 mm mortars the **M74** is moved on a light, two-wheeled carriage; the bipod and baseplate remain attached to the barrel so that it can easily and quickly be brought into action by simply tipping up the carriage until the baseplate rests on the ground, then detaching the carriage and swinging the bipod round into place. When the situation demands, the three components of the mortar can be separated and carried by men or mules

M74 120 mm Light Mortar

into position inaccessible to the wheeled carriage.

The lightness of the mortar does not prevent it reaching a useful range. Two high explosive projectiles are available; a light bomb of 12.6 kg which gives a maximum range of 6200 metres, and a rocket assisted bomb of 13.42 kg which can reach out to 9400 metres. This latter bomb has the rear one-third of the body taken up by a rocket motor which is ignited by a delay unit after firing. Once launched by the normal cartridge, the delay unit first blows off the cartridge container and then the rocket motor ignites and boosts the velocity to increase the maximum range. However, it is also possible to fire this bomb with the rocket motor ignition system disabled, so that it becomes a conventional bomb with a maximum range of 5350 metres. This is somewhat less than the light bomb but has the advantage of carrying a heavier weight of TNT so that the destructive effect is greater. The rocket assistance is also valuable in lifting the maximum altitude of the bomb trajectory, another useful feature in mountainous country.

Other bombs available for this mortar include white phosphorous smoke, hexachlorethane persistent smoke and an illuminating bomb which carries a parachute and flare capable of delivering 900,000 candle-power for 50 seconds, illuminating an area some 1800 metres in diameter.

Specification

Calibre: 120 mm

Elevation: 45° to 85°

Traverse: 6° right and left

Weight in firing position: 120 kg

Maximum range: 9055 m

Minimum range: 265 m

Maximum muzzle velocity: 266 m/sec

Rate of fire: 12 rounds/min

Manufacturer: Federal Supply Bureau,
Yugoslavia

Near Right: The rocket-assisted bomb for the Yugoslavian M74/75 mortars. The high explosive bursting charge occupies the forward part of the bomb body, and the solid-fuel rocket motor occupies the rear, with the tail unit and cartridge container behind. These are discarded after firing to allow the rocket blast to escape.

Far Right: The M74 mortar, packed on its travelling carriage and with the rocket-assisted bomb in front.

HOTCHKISS MCB-81 81 mm Gun-Mortar France

The gun-mortar was developed in the 1970s by Thomson-Brandt as a simple means of arming an armoured car; it began as a short-barrelled weapon which could be muzzle-loaded from the turret hatch, but then it was given a breech-loading facility for use when muzzle-loading exposed the gunner to danger. From this it moved to a longer barrel and higher velocity, until now the 81 mm version (there are also 60 mm models) is a highly efficient dual-purpose weapon. It can be breech-or muzzle-loaded as a low pressure mortar and fired at high angles, or it can be breech-loaded as a medium-pressure gun and fired at flat trajectories.

The gun-mortar is mounted in a hydro-pneumatic recoil system and fits into the turret of most armoured cars and APCs.

As a muzzle-loaded mortar it can fire the entire standard range of French 81 mm high explosive, smoke and illuminating bombs, having a maximum range of 8000 metres when firing the 7.1 kg long range bomb. In this use the firing pin is locked forward and the bomb is drop-fired in the usual manner. When used as a breech-loading mortar the breech is opened and the standard bomb loaded into the barrel, after which the breech is closed and the cocked firing pin is released to ignite the normal mortar charge.

As a breech-loading gun, the **MCB-81** is provided with an armour-piercing, fin-stabilised, discarding sabot projectile carried in a combustible cartridge with a short metal base. This is loaded just like any artillery ammunition, the breech closed, and the cartridge fired to send the projectile from the muzzle at 1000 metres per second. It is capable of penetrating 90 mm of armour plate at 1000 metres range, giving the armoured car or APC a very useful degree of protection against light armoured vehicles.

Gun-mortars can also be mounted on light patrol craft for river patrolling or as support for raiding parties. As well as being operated by the French army they have been sold to a number of other countries, and the design has been also manufactured in South Africa.

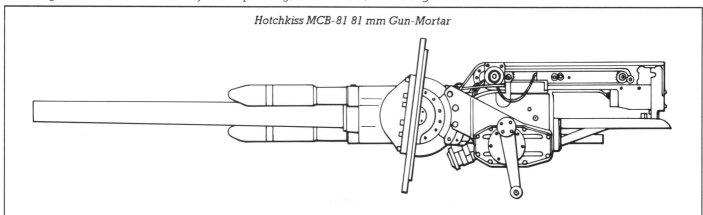

Hotchkiss MCB-81 81 mm Gun-Mortar

Specification

Calibre: 81 mm

Elevation: -10° to +70°

Traverse: 360° in turret mount

Weight in firing position: 400 kg

Maximum range: 8000 m

Minimum range: 100 m

Maximum muzzle velocity: 1000 m/sec (APFSDS)

Rate of fire: 30 rounds/min

Manufacturer: Thomson-Brandt
Armement, France

The Hotchkiss-Brandt 81 mm gun-mortar mounted in the turret of an armoured reconnaissance vehicle, giving it the ability to engage targets by direct or indirect fire.

STRIX Anti-tank Guided Mortar Projectile   Sweden

The **Strix** guided mortar projectile, developed by Bofors in conjunction with Saab Missiles, is another attempt to provide the infantry with a method of attacking armour which is not within a direct line of sight and thus cannot be engaged by the usual missiles or launchers.

Strix is fired from the standard types of 120 mm smooth-bore mortar, and is handled like any other mortar ammunition, being drop-loaded into the mortar. It is supplied in three parts, the guided bomb, the tail unit which carries the propelling charge and an optional sustainer rocket motor. For firing at ranges up to 5000 metres, the tail unit is assembled to **Strix** and the complete unit is then loaded and fired. For ranges from 5000 to 7500 metres the optional sustainer rocket is attached; this ignites during the upward portion of flight and thus extends the range; once burned out it is automatically discarded.

During the descent of the weapon an infra-red seeker in the nose is switched on and scans the area beneath the bomb; it can be programmed before launch to recognise specific types of target from their infra-red signatures, and once it acquires a target with the required features the seeker locates it and informs the guidance system. This then calculates a course and, by firing side-thruster rockets in the central body of the weapon, steers it on course to the selected target. Correction continues up to the moment of impact. The rear of the weapon body carries a powerful shaped charge warhead, which, due to the length of the weapon, is at the correct stand-off distance when the nose impacts the target and an impact fuze initiates the charge. Since this weapon is attacking the vulnerable upper surfaces, it can destroy any known type of armoured vehicle.

Strix has been adopted by the Swedish army and is the first autonomous mortar guided projectile to go into large scale production.

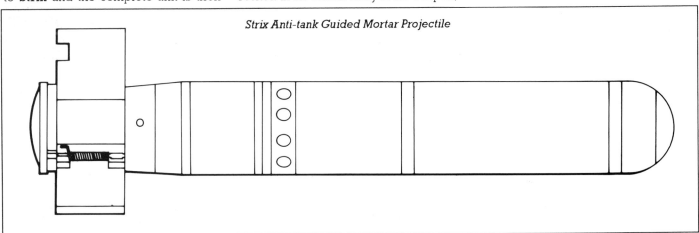

Strix Anti-tank Guided Mortar Projectile

Specification

Guidance: Infra-red seeker

Warhead diameter: 120 mm

Warhead weight:

Launch unit weight:

Missile weight: 18.2 kg

Missile length: 842 mm

Max effective range: 7500 m

Max velocity:

Penetration of armour: >700 mm

Manufacturer: Bofors Weapon Systems,
Sweden

Loading Strix into the 120 mm mortar. The tail unit and propelling charge are separately loaded first, and the terminally guided munition component is loaded after it.

BUSSARD Anti-tank Mortar Projectile   Germany

Guided missiles and other launchers, such as have been already described, all rely upon the firer being within sight of his target, which is not much help to an infantryman who knows that the enemy is assembling a force of armour on the other side of a hill. Conventional mortar bombs will reach the target but will do very little damage. It was to address this problem that the Diehl company of Germany developed the 'Bussard' (buzzard) guided mortar projectile.

Development of this weapon began in 1975 at the request of the German Defence Ministry, and the aim of the work was to produce a guided weapon which could be launched from existing ordnance without demanding modification to the ordnance or complicated guidance apparatus.

Bussard consists of a shaped charge warhead, a central body with power supplies and guidance controls, a seeker head and a tail unit. Designed to be compatible with the standard German 120 mm mortar, the complete unit is loaded and fired from the mortar exactly as any other conventional bomb. After firing, and during the upward flight of the weapon, a thermal battery is activated and a gyroscope is run up to speed. At the peak of its trajectory the wings are folded outwards, power is supplied to the flight controls, and the laser seeking head is activated. On the ground, the target must be illuminated by a laser designator; this can be done by an observer on the ground or from a helicopter or fixed-wing aircraft. As the Bussard descends, the laser energy reflected from the target is detected by the seeker, the position of the target is determined, and the control system then actuates the wing and tail surfaces to steer the weapon towards the target with an accuracy of half a metre. Once aligned on an impact course the warhead may be activated by a proximity fuze or the weapon may be allowed to continue so as to detonate on impact.

For situations where laser illumination would be difficult or inappropriate, alternative seeker heads using millimetric radar or passive infra-red have also been developed.

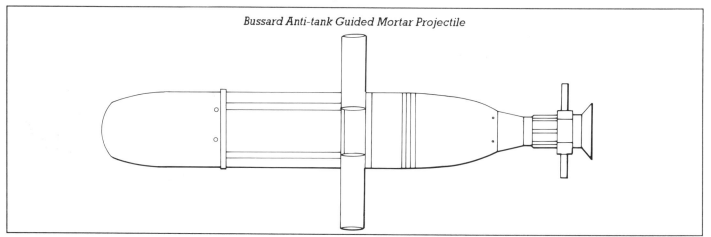

Bussard Anti-tank Guided Mortar Projectile

Specification

Guidance: laser/radar/IR seeker

Warhead diameter: 120 mm

Warhead weight:

Launch unit weight:

Missile weight: 17 kg

Missile length: 1000 mm

Max effective range: 5000 m

Max velocity:

Manufacturer: Diehl GmbH Germany

Downward trajectory of the Bussard projectile about to hit target.

MERLIN 81 mm Guided Mortar Projectile UK

Merlin is a terminally-guided 81 mm mortar bomb which carries a shaped charge for the top attack of armoured vehicles. Other weapons of this type are in the 120 mm calibre, and compressing the necessary guidance, controls and warhead into this smaller bomb has been a difficult task which has proved a great success. It was developed as a private venture by British Aerospace in the early 1980s; once they had shown that their ideas were workable, it was formally backed by the Ministry of Defence, and production for service began in late 1994.

Firing is performed in the normal manner, drop-loading the bomb into the mortar. After it leaves the muzzle six fins spring out into the air at the tail, and four canard wings spring out from the centre of the bomb. A millimetric-wave radar seeker in the nose is switched on as the bomb approaches the highest point of the trajectory, and as it descends the seeker begins searching for targets, scanning an area about 300 metres square. It is programmed to first seek moving targets; then, if it finds none, it seeks stationary targets. Having acquired a target it locks on to it and a computer calculates the angular correction necessary to direct the trajectory towards the target. Commands are issued to the four canard wings and the bomb is steered into a new path, corrections being constantly recalculated

as the bomb closes with the target. On impact, the shaped charge is fired, penetrating the armour on the upper surface of the target. It is sufficiently powerful to penetrate a main battle tank and will completely destroy lighter vehicles such as personnel carriers.

Work is in progress to develop a similar bomb in 120 mm calibre, and the seeker and control system is being adapted to an air-launched anti-armour rocket projectile. Merlin can be fired from any smoothbore 81 mm mortar, and a simple alteration in the plastic sealing ring will allow it to be fired from various 82 mm mortars used in foreign armies.

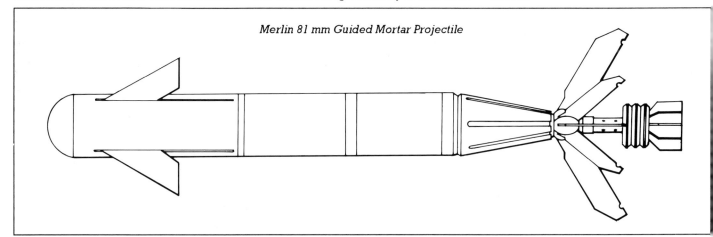

Merlin 81 mm Guided Mortar Projectile

Specification:

Guidance: Millimetric wave radar seeker

Warhead diameter: 81 mm

Missile weight: 6.5 kg

Missile length: 900 mm

Max effective range: 4000 m

Penetration of armour: Not disclosed

Manufacturer: British Aerospace
Dynamics

Loading the Merlin terminally guided mortar munition into the standard British 81 mm mortar L16. In spite of its advanced technology, Merlin is handled and fired just like any other mortar bomb.

Ammunition

No weapon is of very much use without ammunition, which is perhaps why some people cling to the bayonet. It is also true to say that the best way to improve a weapon is to improve its ammunition, and this is a course which has been emphasised in the past two decades. In that time we have progressed from simple 'iron' munitions to far-from-simple 'smart' munitions, munitions which, once released from the gun, can seek out their own targets, or which can carry other munitions inside and scatter them over a target, area, so multiplying the chance of lethal hit by a considerable factor. Instead of simple fuzes which react to the impact on the target there are fuzes which detect the presence of a target in the vicinity, measure its distance, decide when it is within the lethal striking area of the munition, and detonate it at the most effective point. No longer need a simple box of explosives be buried in a track and wait for a tank to drive over it; today's mine will lie in wait at the roadside, sense the passage of the tank, and fire a missile at it as it passes. It can even be programmed to ignore one or two dozen vehicles before going into action. The infantryman's armoury has been vastly increased not only by new weapons but by ingenious developments in the ammunition for those weapons.

A conventional 120 mm mortar.It has a plastic gas-sealing ring around its waist. The propellant is packed in cloth bags which slip around the tail tube and are ignited by a shotgun type cartridge. When the bomb is dropped down the barrel, this cartridge strikes the firing pin and the flash ignites the bags of powder.

A 120 mm mortar bomb for a rifled mortar. The driving band already has the rifling grooves and thus has to be carefully loaded so that the rifling in the barrel fits into these grooves. After firing, the tail unit drops off, and the bomb spins in flight like a gun shell.

A shaped charged mortar bomb. This can be used with a conventional mortar so as to drop on the thinner top surfaces of a tank or fired from a gun mortar at side armour.

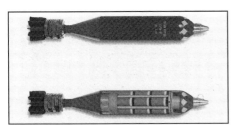

The Spanish 'Espin' sub-munition bomb. A 120 mm bomb, it carries 21 bomblets inside, which are released above the target area. The target in question being a force of armoured vehicles preparing for an attack, it is unlikely that they will escape scot-free from a few of these bombs being fired at them.

The inside of a typical 40 mm shaped charge grenade. Notice the large amount of space behind the charge which is taken up by the fuze. Note also the 'High - Low Pressure System' cartridge, in which the propellant is enclosed in a tiny chamber over the cap, and the gas allowed to bleed into the empty space in the cartridge, to provide a low - pressure, low - recoil force to eject the grenade.

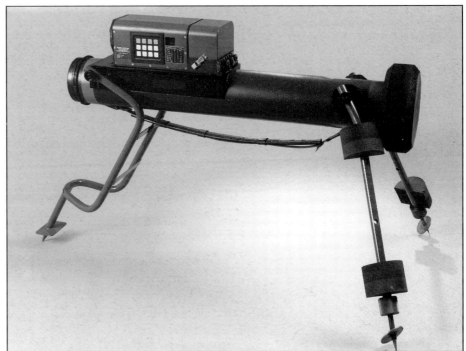

An alternative use for an anti-tank rocket launcher. Place it on a stand and fit it with a sensor which will detect a passing tank. A computer will assess the course and range and fire the rocket at the correct moment to connect with the target. What you have is an 'off-route mine' which can be concealed near a road and left to its own devices.

GLF-90 Multiple Grenade Launcher   Italy

This is an unusual weapon, intended to allow rifle grenades to be fired to their maximum range without requiring a rifle and also to improve the accuracy by using a rather more precise and stable firing device than a hand-held rifle. In effect, it is a pair of very short barrels mounted so as to be capable of precise elevation and traverse. It can be made with barrels to suit either the 5.56 x 45 mm cartridge or the 7.62 x 51 mm cartridge, and the range obtainable depends entirely upon which cartridge is used and which particular make of grenade is selected.

Any NATO-standard grenade with a 22 mm tail tube can be fired, the maximum range depending upon the weight of the grenade. The barrels are not rifled and are bored so as to be wider at the muzzle than at the breech end, though the exterior is parallel. To fire, a blank cartridge is simply dropped base first down the barrel and the grenade tail slipped over the barrel. On pulling the firing lever a pin goes through a hole in the bottom of the barrel and fires the blank cartridge; the propellant gas then launches the grenade. Gas pressure also forces the

cartridge case back, but it is not a tight fit, and a proportion of gas leaks out through the firing pin hole, into a chamber in the baseplate, rebounds, and then goes back through the hole to add to the propulsive force. This initial blast of gas downward into the baseplate tends to stabilise it and anchor it firmly for the brief period of the grenade's launch, and it is a patented feature of the design.

At the present time the **GLF-90** is under evaluation by a number of military forces.

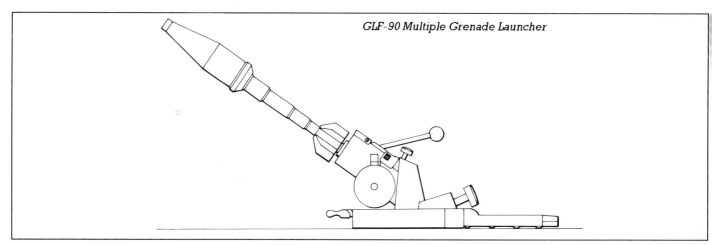

GLF-90 Multiple Grenade Launcher

Specification

Projectile: Any NATO-standard rifle grenade

Weight, empty: 8 kg

Dimensions folded: 460 x 400 x 200 mm

Elevation: 15° to 75°

Traverse: 10° either side of zero

Maximum range: 600 - 900 m

Manufacturer: Luigi Franchi SpA, Italy

Rear view of the GLF-90 launcher with two rifle grenades loaded. The two levers control the breeches, the knobs control elevation, traverse and safety.

CIS 40-AGL Auto. Grenade Launcher   Singapore

This is an air-cooled blowback weapon firing the standard type of high-velocity 40 mm grenade to a maximum range of 2200 metres. It can be mounted on a tripod for direct infantry support, or on a variety of vehicular, turret or boat mountings.

The gun operates in the blowback mode, using advanced primer ignition. The grenades are carried in a link belt, feeding from the left of the gun, and when the bolt is cocked and held back, the belt is advanced half a cartridge width. On pressing the trigger the bolt is released; as it goes forward the belt is advanced a further half-cartridge width, so bringing the cartridge into the feed position, from where it is rammed into the chamber by the bolt. Just before the round is fully chambered, and while the bolt is still moving forwards, the firing pin is released to fire the grenade cartridge. The explosion force thus has to arrest the moving mass of the bolt before it can begin to drive it backwards, and this allows a lighter bolt and shorter bolt stroke than would be possible if the bolt was allowed to come to a stop before firing. As the bolt is driven back it extracts and ejects the cartridge case to the right of the weapon, and at the same time moves the belt a half-step, and the whole cycle is then repeated for each shot.

The 40 mm cartridge operates on the High-Low Pressure principle. The cartridge case has a strong inner chamber surrounding the area in front of the cap, and the propellant is inside this chamber. The chamber has a number of small holes leading into the body of the cartridge case, which is empty. On firing, the propellant burns at very high pressure inside this chamber, and the gas is bled out into the empty space within the case, there to expand and provide a low-pressure thrust to the grenade. This relieves the grenade of considerable firing stress and also reduces the recoil on the weapon.

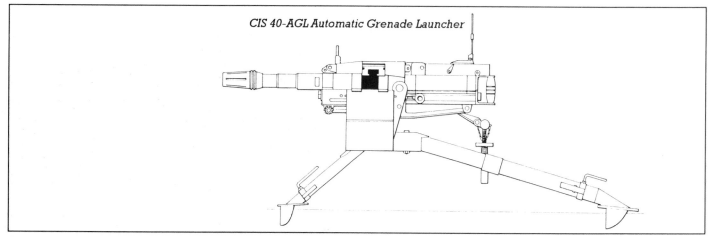

CIS 40-AGL Automatic Grenade Launcher

Specification

Projectile: 40 x 53 mm high velocity grenade

Operating system: Blowback

Weight, empty: 33 kg

Length overall: 966 mm

Barrel: 350 mm

Feed system: Disintegrating link belt

Rate of Fire: 350 rounds/min

Muzzle velocity: 241 m/sec

Maximum range: 2200 m

Manufacturer: Chartered Industries of Singapore, Singapore

Above Right: The Singapore designed CIS 40 AGL grenade launcher on its ground bipod, with the ammunition belt feed box in place.
Below Right: The CIS 40 AGL launcher mounted in the turret of a light armoured vehicle. Reloading under fire might prove trying for the crew.

ARMSCOR MGL 6-shot Grenade Launcher   S. Africa

This weapon uses the revolver principle to provide a fast-firing hand-held weapon which can fire all types of 40 mm low-velocity grenade. It consists of a light rifled barrel, frame and firing mechanism, spring-driven revolving chamber, folding butt and sight unit.

The weapon is loaded by releasing a catch and swinging the rear of the frame away from the cylinder. The firer then puts his fingers into the empty chambers and winds the cylinder operating spring by turning the cylinder against a ratchet. He then loads the six chambers with grenades, swings back the frame and locks it. The sight is an 'Occluded Eye

Gunsight' which can be used with both eyes open; it then appears to project a red spot on to the target. It also has a range-finding capability, and can be adjusted in 25-metres range steps. The sight also makes automatic compensation for the sideways drift of the projectile.

The trigger is a self-cocking mechanism which cocks and releases the firing pin, firing the grenade which is positioned behind the barrel. A gas piston, actuated by a portion of the propellant gas behind the grenade, unlocks the cylinder and allows the spring to drive it round until the next chamber is aligned with the barrel,

where it is automatically locked. During this movement the firing mechanism cannot operate, but as soon as the cylinder is locked the trigger can be pulled for another shot. Shots can be fired at one-second intervals, and reloading is relatively swift once the firer has had some practice, so that 18 to 20 rounds per minute can be easily reached and maintained.

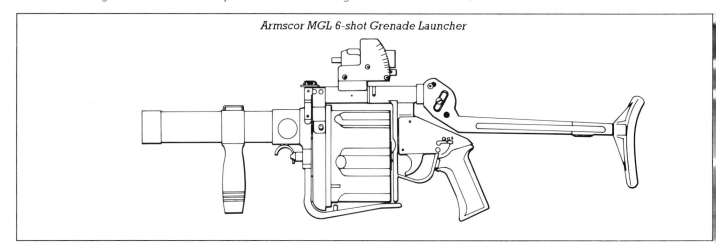

Armscor MGL 6-shot Grenade Launcher

Specification

Projectile: 40 x 46 mm low velocity grenade

Weight, empty: 5.3 kg

Length overall: 788 mm butt extended; 566 mm butt folded

Barrel: 310 mm, 6 grooves, rh, increasing twist

Feed system: Six-shot cylinder

Rate of Fire: 18-20 rounds/min

Muzzle velocity: 76 m/sec

Manufacturer: Armscor, South Africa

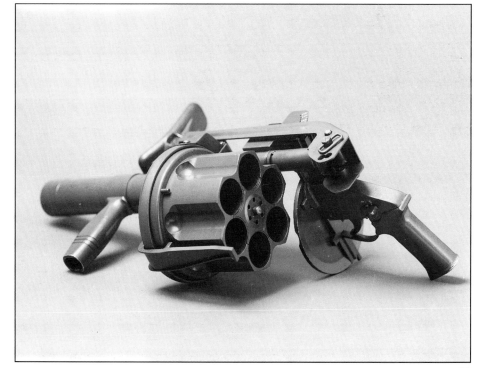

The Armscor grenade launcher swung open to expose the rear end of the cylinder for loading.

GP-25 40 mm Grenade Launcher F. Soviet Union

This weapon was first seen in Afghanistan in 1984 and is fairly obviously based upon the US Army M203 grenade launcher, fitting beneath the barrel of the standard Kalashnikov AK-series rifles.

The **GP-25** is a short rifled barrel of 40 mm calibre fitted with a trigger and a short hand-grip. The grenade is inserted into the muzzle base first, the firer takes aim, and the trigger is pulled. This cocks and releases the firing pin and fires the propelling charge in the base of the grenade. There is no cartridge case; the rear of the grenade is shaped to form a chamber for the propellant and has a primer fitted centrally. This chamber has holes around its periphery, covered by

a driving band, and more holes in the base which are normally sealed by a thin plastic disc. On firing, the gas pressure passes through these holes; those at the rear provide the thrust to drive the grenade forward, while those under the driving band allow gas to force the band outwards to grip the rifling of the barrel and spin the grenade to stabilise it in flight.

The launcher has a simple sight which is adjustable to the maximum range of 400 metres. At this range the weapon is claimed to deliver the grenade within a rectangle 3 m wide and 6 m long.

There are two types of grenade provided. The VOG-25 is a high explosive/fragmentation grenade with an

impact fuze and carries a charge of 48 grammes of explosive; the VOG-25P is of the same type, but has an additional feature; the nose is longer and contains a small charge of smokeless powder and an impact cap. On striking the ground, this cap fires the powder charge and this blows the grenade back up into the air. As it does this, it also ignites a very short delay, which, when the grenade has risen about 1.5 metres into the air, detonates the high explosive charge. This ensures that none of the fragments are smothered by the ground and all spread out at a lethal height around the point of burst. This, however, is rarely effective on soft ground.

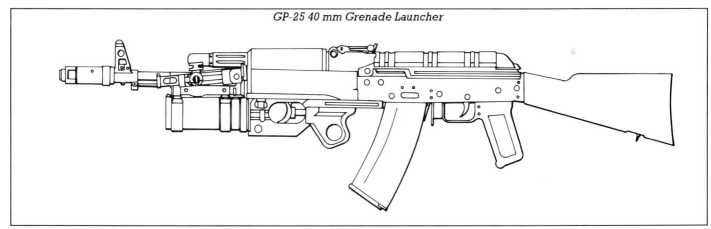

GP-25 40 mm Grenade Launcher

Specification

Cartridge: 40 mm VOG

Weight, empty: 1.79 kg loaded

Length overall: 325 mm

Barrel: 120 mm

Feed system: Single shot

Maximum range: 420 m

Muzzle velocity: 77 m/sec

Manufacturer: State arsenals, Former Soviet Union

An Afghan guerrilla demonstrating one of the first BG-15 grenade launchers seen outside the FSU. It is attached to an AK-74 rifle by a special kit and, as he shows, can be very easily fired by the forward hand without losing grip of the rifle.

AGS-17 Grenade Launcher F. Soviet Union

The **AGS-17** grenade launcher was introduced into Soviet service in 1975 but was rarely seen before its use in the Afghanistan campaign. It is issued to infantry companies, and has also been seen mounted in helicopters and on various light armoured vehicles.

The weapon operates on a simple blowback system. The ammunition is belt-fed into the right side of the receiver, and the bolt is cocked by pulling back an operating handle at the rear of the weapon. This is attached to the bolt by a steel cable. When this is pulled back and released, the bolt is drawn back against a return spring and then propelled forward to collect a round from the belt and load it into the chamber. The firer then takes aim, holding the weapon by two spade grips at the rear, and presses a trigger fitted between the grips. This releases the firing pin to fire the cartridge and eject the grenade. The gas pressure in the breech presses back the bolt, overcoming the inertia due to its weight, and blows it backwards until it is stopped by a buffer in the end of the receiver. The empty cartridge case is ejected from the bottom of the gun, and a feed arm attached to the bolt moves the ammunition belt across to position the next round. The bolt then returns, collecting the fresh round and chambering it ready for the next shot. If the weapon is set for automatic fire, the firing pin is released as soon as the bolt has closed.

The standard infantry mounting is a tripod with mechanical elevation and traversing gears. An optical panoramic sight is fitted on the left side of the receiver, and on top of the receiver is a plate giving angles of elevation for various ranges.

The grenade fired by this weapon is the 30 mm VOG-17M, a high explosive/fragmentation grenade fitted with an impact fuze which has a self-destruction device which detonates the grenade after 25 seconds of flight. The grenade body is of light metal and is lined internally with a layer of hard wax into which several hundred steel balls are inserted. The space inside this fragmentation liner is filled with explosive. The cartridge case is short, of steel, and is simply a container for a charge of smokeless powder and a percussion cap; there is no propellant combustion control as in the American 40 mm design.

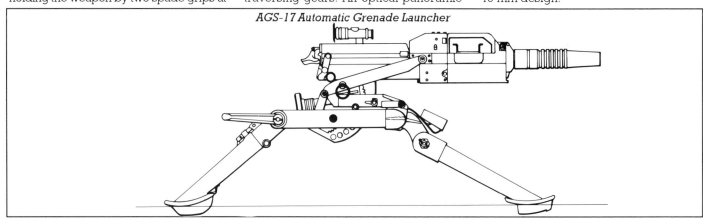

AGS-17 Automatic Grenade Launcher

Specification

Calibre: 30 mm

Operating system: Blowback

Weight, empty: 18 kg gun; 35 kg tripod

Length overall: 840 mm

Barrel: 290 mm, 16 grooves, rh

Feed system: 29-round belt

Rate of Fire: 65 rounds/min

Muzzle velocity: 853 m/sec

Manufacturer: State arsenals, Former Soviet Union

Two Russian soldiers preparing their AGS-17 grenade launcher for firing. One is cocking the bolt by means of a wire strop and toggle, while the other loads the belt into the gun and arranges the ammunition in the belt box.

LAG-40 Automatic Grenade Launcher   Spain

The **LAG-40** is a Spanish design which illustrates a different method of firing the 40 mm high-velocity grenade so as to reduce the recoil and thus allow the weapon to be light enough to be easily handled; it also has a desirable side-effect in reducing the rate of fire to 215 rounds per minute, which is tactically preferable to the more usual 350-400 figure.

The weapon operates on the long recoil principle in which the breech and barrel recoil locked together for a distance of about six inches inside the outer casing of the weapon. They then stop, the bolt is unlocked and held, and the barrel runs forward to the firing position. During this movement the cartridge case is extracted and ejected and the feed mechanism places a fresh cartridge in the feedway. As the barrel comes to rest, it releases a catch which allows the bolt to run forward, driven by a spring. It collects the round in the feedway, places it in the chamber, and then locks into the barrel, after which the firing pin is released and the grenade is fired.

The very long travel of the bolt, against its buffer and return springs, allows the mounting to absorb the recoil over a longer period of time, and the delay imposed by the independent movements of bolt and barrel produce a slower rate of fire than does a blowback system.

Another unusual feature of the **LAG-40** is its ability to feed from either side of the weapon, the belt feed mechanism being easily convertible without the use of tools. This gives the weapon a wide versatility and allows it to be mounted in vehicles, boats or on a tripod.

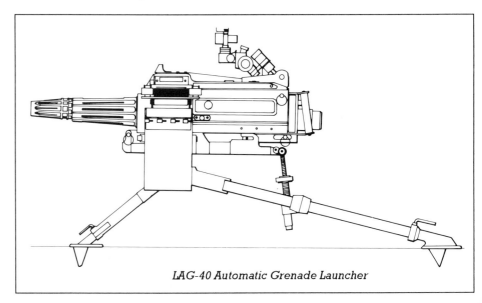

LAG-40 Automatic Grenade Launcher

Specification

Projectile: 40 x 53 mm high velocity grenade

Operating system: Long recoil

Weight, empty: 34 kg gun; 22 kg tripod

Length overall: 996 mm

Barrel: 415 mm: 18 grooves, rh

Feed system: 24- or 32-round linked belt

Rate of Fire: 215 rounds/min

Muzzle velocity: 240 m/sec

Maximum range: 1500 m

Manufacturer: Santa Barbara, Spain

A two-man team of the Spanish Army firing the LAG-40 grenade launcher.

RAAM

The **RAAM** project (Rifle-launched Anti-armour Munition) began in response to a 1990 US Army requirement for a rifle-fired anti-armour weapon. Two companies, the Olin Corporation and McDonnell Douglas, developed solutions, both of which were essentially over-sized rifle grenades using a shaped charge warhead. Recent (March 1995) information indicates that the McDonnell Douglas project has been abandoned, due to the company pulling out of the ground weapons field, and that only the Olin design continues in an advanced stage of development.

The Olin RAAM is a rocket-boosted bullet-trap rifle grenade using a tandem shaped charge warhead. It can be fired from any M16A2 rifle by means of a plastic expendable adapter which is slipped over the rifle's muzzle, the grenade tail then being slipped over the adapter. The rifle is fired, using a standard ball bullet; this is trapped inside the tail unit of the RAAM and the combination of the blow from the bullet and the propellant gas pressure launches the projectile off the rifle. The rocket is then ignited and the projectile accelerates down-range. This combination of grenade-style launch followed by rocket boost means there is no danger to the firer from back-blast and the **RAAM** can be safely fired from inside a building or other confined space. Launching from a rifle also gives the weapon a much lower firing signature than most comparable shoulder-launched weapons.

On impact the two shaped charges fire in rapid succession; the first charge will remove any reactive armour which may be fitted to the target, leaving the basic armour exposed to attack by the second charge. Where there is no reactive or other applied armour, then the first charge will make a hole part-way through the armour which will then be completed by the second charge. Attacking light armour - APCs and the like - with a warhead of this nature ensures devastating damage to the inside of the vehicle.

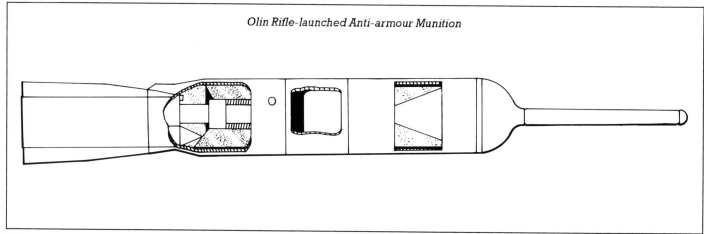

Olin Rifle-launched Anti-armour Munition

Specification

Weight in firing order: 1.65 kg

Maximum range: 250 m

Penetration of armour: >400 mm

Manufacturer: Olin Corp. USA

*A rifleman about to fire an Olin RAA munition
from his M16A1 rifle.*

Rifleman's Assault Weapon (RAW)   USA

Although launched from a rifle, the **RAW** has an effect at the target comparable with a light artillery shell. It was developed as a weapon for use in urban warfare where an enemy can be protected by sandbags or strong walls in positions where it is not possible to bring a tank or artillery piece to bear. In such cases a sizeable charge is necessary to blow a hole in the protection, and the usual rifle grenades are not sufficiently powerful for the task.

RAW is a rocket-propelled projectile launched from the muzzle of a rifle. The warhead is 140 mm diameter and contains 2.2 lbs of plastic explosive. On impact, the casing is broken and the plastic explosive is plastered on to the target and then detonated by a base fuze. The force of the detonation wave will blow a hole 360 mm in diameter in 200 mm thickness of reinforced concrete. Alternative warheads include an anti-personnel fragmenting type which blasts several thousand tungsten pellets around the point of detonation, and a shaped charge warhead which will defeat armour plate.

The projectile is a metal sphere with a rocket nozzle. A special launcher is clipped below the rifle's muzzle and the projectile placed on it. The firer loads a normal ball cartridge and pulls the trigger. A collar around the rifle muzzle deflects some of the gas emerging behind the bullet and directs it through a tube to the launcher, where it impinges on a firing pin and fires a cap in the base of the rocket nozzle. This ignites the projectile rocket, and the first blast passes into the launcher tube and drives a turbine, spinning the tube and thus spinning the projectile as the rocket thrust propels it from the launcher. The projectile flies off with constant acceleration and, since it is spun and not fin-stabilised, it is very accurate and does not turn into the wind as does a finned projectile. There is very little back-blast at launch, and the firer feels only slightly more recoil than he would from firing a normal ball round. The **RAW** is now in limited production for US forces.

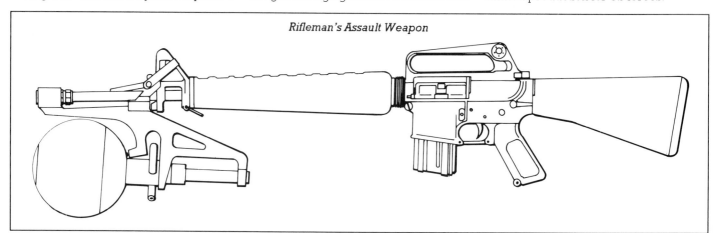

Rifleman's Assault Weapon

Specification

Calibre of warhead: 140 mm

Weight in firing order: 4.73 kg

Length of launcher: 305 mm

Maximum range: 1500 m

Maximum velocity: 173 m/sec

Penetration of concrete: >200 mm

Manufacturer: Brunswick Corp. USA

A US infantryman takes aim with the Brunswick RAW. Because of the rocket propulsion system, most of the recoil he will feel will come from the rifle bullet which he fires to ignite the rocket.

M203 Grenade Launcher

The idea of an automatic grenade launcher occurred to the US Army very quickly after their **M203** under-barrel single-shot launcher was introduced into Vietnam in the 1960s, and one or two designs were developed and tested. But by the time they were working, the Vietnam war was over and there seemed no tactical purpose in the idea, so it was given low priority. Then, in the mid-1970s, the Soviet 30 mm launcher 'Plamya' was revealed, and suddenly automatic grenade launchers were a desirable weapon. The Mark 19 Mod 3 was developed by the US Naval Ordnance and production was by the Saco company; it went into service in 1980.

The Mark 19 Mod 3 is an air-cooled blowback machine gun firing high-velocity 40 mm grenades. The weapon fires from the open bolt position, and the forward movement of the bolt also controls the ammunition feed mechanism, indexing a round across into the feedway. As the bolt is cocked it withdraws a round from the ammunition belt, and a vertical curved cam forces the cartridge down the T-slot in the face of the bolt until it is aligned with the chamber. On pulling the trigger, the bolt runs forward and chambers the round, and just before the case is fully seated the firing pin is released, firing the cartridge before the bolt has come to rest. As already described, this means that the explosion pressure has first to stop the bolt and then drive it backwards, and this permits the use of a lighter bolt and thus a lighter weapon.

As the bolt is blown back, so it extracts the empty case from the chamber; at the same time it is withdrawing a fresh round from the belt, and as the vertical cam forces this new round down the T-slot in the bolt face, so it pushes the empty case out of the slot and ejects it through the bottom of the receiver.

Various sighting devices can be used with the Mark 19. It is fitted with a simple aperture backsight and blade foresight as standard, but it is also possible to mount various optical and electro-optical day and night sights, laser target indicators and laser rangefinders to a special bracket which can be adjusted for range.

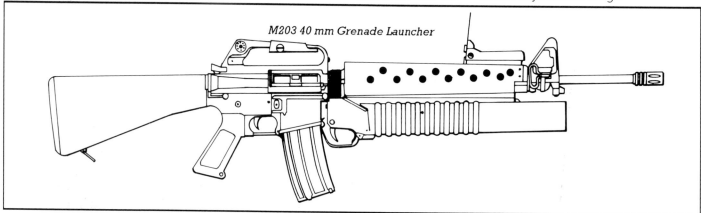

M203 40 mm Grenade Launcher

Specification:

Projectile: 40 x 56 mm high velocity grenade

Operation: Blowback

Weight in firing order: 35.3 kg

Length: 1095 mm

Feed system: 20- or 50-round link belt

Maximum range: 1500 m

Muzzle velocity: 241 m/sec

Rate of fire: 350 rounds/min

Manufacturer: Saco Inc

Above: *The product-improved M203 grenade launcher fitted to the Austrian Steyr AUG rifle; with suitable adaptors it can be fitted to almost any assault rifle currently in use.*

Centre: *The product-improved M203 can be used by itself fitted to a simple supporting frame and folding stock.*

Below: *A sectioned example of the standard M406 40 mm high explosive/fragmentation grenade used with the M203 launcher. The notched sphere is the actual grenade body, the components in front are the fuze.*

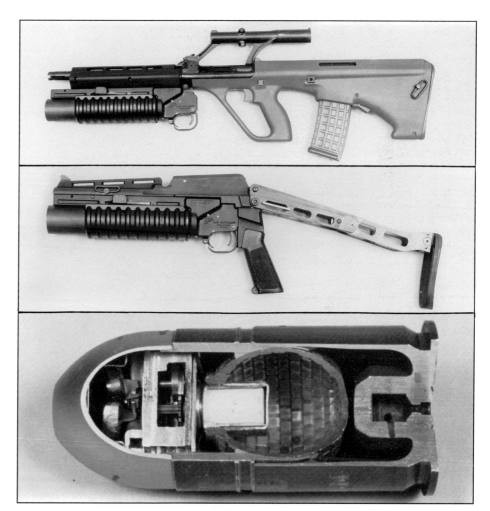

Rifle Grenades

Firing a grenade from a rifle extends the range considerably; few people can throw a grenade much further than 30 metres, but a rifle will send one out to over 400 metres. Rocket - assisted grenades, of which there are a few, will reach out to 700 metres. Almost all modern rifles outside the Soviet sphere of influence have standardised on a 22 mm diameter for rifle muzzles, and modern grenades are made to suit, so that grenades and rifles are widely interchangeable. Years ago it was necessary to use a special blank cartridge to provide the power, but most grenades today are of the 'bullet-trap' kind which allow the soldier to use whatever cartridge happens to be in the chamber of his rifle. The tail unit of the grenade carries a special steel trap which arrests the bullet. The impact starts the grenade moving and the expanding gap behind the bullet supplies the thrust. As with hand grenades, the standard missile is a high explosive/fragmentation pattern, and smoke grenades are also commonly provided. But in addition the comparatively flat trajectory of a rifle grenade allows a side-on shot against vehicles, so shaped charge anti-armour rifle grenades are very popular. Since the weight of a rifle grenade is severely limited (otherwise it would have very little range and the recoil would damage the rifle) they do not have sufficient power to take on main battle tanks, but they can certainly make life very unpleasant for armoured personnel carriers and similar lightly armoured vehicles.

A Belgian grenade which is somewhat different, since it allows the propelling rifle bullet to pass completely through a central tube instead of trapping it. Note the rear grenade has a tail unit extended into the firing position and the sight (which is part of the grenade, not the rifle) raised.

Top Right: Firing the Belgian 'Bullet Thru' grenade. Once it has left the rifle the tail unit will slide back into the body, arming the grenade so that it will detonate on impact. The telescoping design makes for a compact unit when carried; note the grenade container on the soldier's belt.

Near Right: A French shaped charge anti-tank grenade . It has a maximum range of 350 m and can defeat 200 mm of armour plate.

Centre Right: A Belgian bullet-trap grenade on the muzzle of the Austrian AUG rifle. This combination will give a range of about 400 m and produce over 300 lethal fragments to cover a 10 m radius danger circle.

Below Right: A French 'polyvalent' grenade. The head unit can be used as a simple hand grenade or the tail unit can be screwed on to convert it into a rifle grenade. The fuze is also convertible and can be set for a five-second delay for hand-throwing or to operate on impact in the rifle role.

MILAN Anti-tank Missile   France

Milan (Missile d'Infanterie Leger Anti-char) is one of the most successful anti-tank guided missiles, several tens of thousands have been produced, it is used by most NATO and several other armies, and the basic principle has been widely copied.

Milan was developed by the international consortium "Euromissile' led by Aerospatiale of France and including Deutsche Aerospace and British Aerospace. The weapon uses the SACLOS system in which the firer merely keeps his sight on the target and the sight detects the position of the missile relative to this sight line and steers the missile by means of a wire link. The system consists of a firing post, containing the sights and firing controls, and a pre-packed missile in a launch tube. The two are put together, the firer takes aim and fires, and the missile is ejected from the launch tube by a boost motor, after which a sustainer motor takes over and accelerates the missile to the target. It reaches its maximum range of 2000 metres in 12.5 seconds.

Milan has been steadily improved throughout its life, and the current version, Milan 3, is a much more effective system than the original design. The earlier missiles used a simple infra-red flare in the tail for guidance, and this occasionally led to the sight locking on to a decoy flare or a battlefield fire.

In Milan 3 the missile carries a Xenon lamp, flashing in a code sequence; the sight is programmed to accept this code and no other bright source, so that only the missile is recognised and decoys are ignored. The warhead now carries an extended probe tip with a small shaped charge; this detonates any reactive armour protection and thus clears the way for the detonation of the main charge, allowing it to attack the armour of the target directly.

The firing post is now generally fitted with MIRA, the Milan Infra-Red Attachment which gives excellent night vision and is also useful in daylight for searching out camouflaged vehicles by recognising their heat emissions.

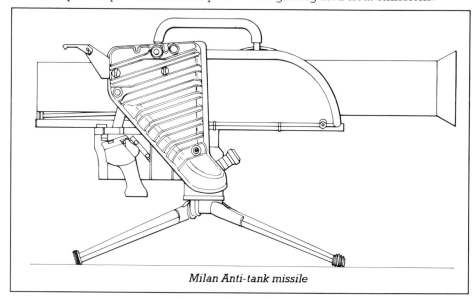

Milan Anti-tank missile

Specification

Guidance: Semi-automatic, wire

Warhead diameter: 133 mm

Warhead weight: 3.12 kg

Launch unit weight: 16.9 kg

Missile weight: 11.91 kg

Missile length: 1200 mm

Max effective range: 2000 m

Max velocity: 210 m/sec

Penetration of armour: >1000 mm

Manufacturer: Aerospatiale-Missiles,
France

Firing the Milan anti-armour missile. The missile is inside the launch tube, still sealed, while the soldier takes aim through the firing post sight, which also contains the tracking optics and fire control electronics.

ERYX Anti-tank Missile

France

One of the drawbacks with anti-tank missiles is that many of them cannot be used at short range, since the missile has to be 'gathered' by the control system and settle down into the line of sight before it can be accurately guided. This limits the range to 500 metres or more, and situations often arise where a tank is at a range where it cannot be engaged by a missile but is too far away for an unguided shoulder-fired launcher to have much chance of hitting. It is to cater for this situation that **Eryx** was developed.

The specification for **Eryx** demanded a weapon with a range of 600 metres, capable of defeating any present-day tank, high accuracy and the ability to fire from enclosed spaces. The result

is a shoulder-fired short range missile using the SACLOS principle of guidance. The missile is pre-packed in a launch and transport tube, and a compact firing unit, which contains the ignition, detection and timing systems, clips on the side of this. The firer attaches the two and places the launcher on his shoulder, takes aim and fires. The missile's flight to maximum range lasts only four seconds, and during this time the firer must keep his sight aligned with his target. As the missile flies, it unreels a control wire attached to the launcher. It also has an infra-red flare in the tail which is 'seen' by the sight; the deviation from the sight axis is measured and corrections computed, and these corrections are signalled down the wire to the missile. In

order to achieve rapid response, the nozzle of the rocket is swivelled so as to change the angle of thrust, a system which gives faster response than altering the angle of wings or other aerodynamic systems.

The use of this 'dynamic thrust control' system also means that the rocket motor can be relatively small, and this also allows the launcher to be fired from inside a building without danger to the firer from the backblast of the rocket during launch.

Eryx was adopted by the French Army, after which it was taken into service by the Canadian and Norwegian armies. It fills a unique slot in the anti-tank armoury and is likely to find a place with other armies in due course.

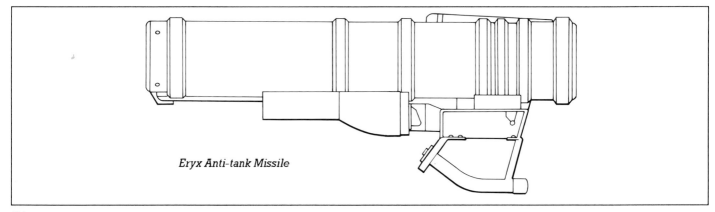

Eryx Anti-tank Missile

Specification

Guidance: Semi-automatic, wire

Warhead diameter: 160 mm

Warhead weight: 3.8 kg

Launch unit weight: 4.5 kg

Missile weight: 12 kg

Missile length: 925 mm

Max. effective range: 600 m

Max. velocity: 300 m/sec

Penetration of armour: 900 mm

Manufacturer: Aerospatiale-Missiles
France

The instant of firing of an Eryx missile from inside a building. The missile is passing through the window, and there is a small cloud of smoke behind the launcher, but no signs of flame or blast to endanger the firer.

PANZERFAUST 3 Anti-tank Launcher   Germany

The German army pioneered the disposable anti-tank launcher during World War Two when they adopted the original Panzerfaust; this was a metal tube in the front of which a projectile with an oversized warhead rested with its tail boom inside the tube. Behind it lay a small charge of gunpowder which, when fired, launched the projectile forwards and delivered a counter-recoil jet from the other end of the tube. The tube was then thrown away.

Although only a short range device the Panzerfaust was death to tanks in 1944-45, and, indeed, still would be today. But more range and precision are demanded today and thus the basic design was considerably improved by Dynamit Nobel when they developed the **Panzerfaust 3** in 1978-85. The weapon consists of a disposable launcher tube carrying a shaped-charge warhead rocket and a re-usable firing and sighting unit. The launch tube is clipped to the firing unit, the firer takes aim and presses the trigger to ignite a propelling charge inside the tube. This ejects the projectile forward and ejects an equivalent counter-mass - a bundle of plastic flakes - to the rear, thus achieving recoillessness. The projectile leaves the launcher at about 165 metres per second velocity, so giving a low firing signature, and the flexible plastic flakes allow the weapon to be fired from an enclosed space since they will be halted without damage when they strike any obstacle. About ten metres after leaving the tube the rocket ignites and accelerates the projectile to about 250 m/sec, and folding fins spring out to stabilise the rocket's flight. An extensible probe in the warhead contacts the target and fires the shaped charge at the optimum stand-off distance to achieve maximum penetration of armour.

The **Panzerfaust 3** can also be set up on a firing post and fitted with various sensors which will allow it to be used as an off-route mine or trap, covering a likely tank route. The sensors (which may be acoustic, infra-red or optical) will detect the presence of a tank and, by means of a computer, calculate the precise firing point so as to hit the target. As many as four weapons can be fitted to one post and will fire in succession or to a pre-set programme.

Panzerfaust 3 was adopted by the German Army in 1987 and has since been purchased by three other armies.

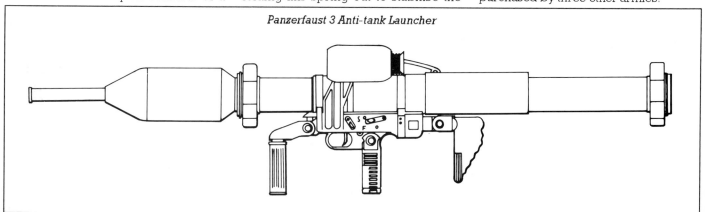

Panzerfaust 3 Anti-tank Launcher

Specification

Calibre of warhead: 110 mm

Weight in firing order: 12.9 kg

Length of launcher: 1200 mm

Maximum range: 500 m stationary target;
300 m moving target

Maximum velocity: 243 m/sec

Penetration of armour: >700 mm

Manufacturer: Dynamit Nobel AG,
Germany

Taking aim with the Panzerfaust 3. Note the large size of the warhead in comparison with the launch tube, and the extended probe on the warhead which ensures detonation of the charge at the optimum distance from the armour.

FOLGORE Anti-tank System   Italy

The Italian Army, when demanding an anti-tank weapon for their light infantry, pointed out that firstly they wanted something which was simple and cheap enough to be liberally distributed, and secondly that they wanted it to have more range than the usual type of shoulder-fired launcher. The Breda company went away and thought about it, and returned with 'Folgore', a recoilless gun light enough to be shoulder-fired and which launches a rocket-boosted shell.

Folgore (which means 'thunderbolt') is a conventional breech-loaded recoilless gun, and the projectile comes with a small cartridge attached to its base.

The round is loaded and fired. The propelling cartridge is relatively low-powered, sufficient to eject the projectile from the muzzle and give it flight speed; at the same time a proportion of the cartridge explosion gas is directed rearwards through a venturi to provide the recoilless effect. After a few metres of flight the rocket ignites and accelerates the projectile to the target; it takes a mere 2.5 seconds to reach 1000 metres. Six fins are deployed after launch so as to stabilise the projectile, and a safety system ensures that the weapon is not armed until a certain level of acceleration has been achieved. Fuzing is electrical, and the nose of the projectile is a double-skinned system in which the two skins are electrically charged; as soon as the nose strikes the target and the two skins are driven into contact, the shaped charge warhead is fired.

Folgore is made in two versions, tripod and bipod-mounted. The weapon is the same in each case, the difference being in the sighting system. The tripod version uses an electronic rangefinding sight and is intended for use in defensive positions to the maximum range of the system. The bipod version uses a simple optical sight, is lighter, and is used in offensive operations where long range is less important than rapidity of response.

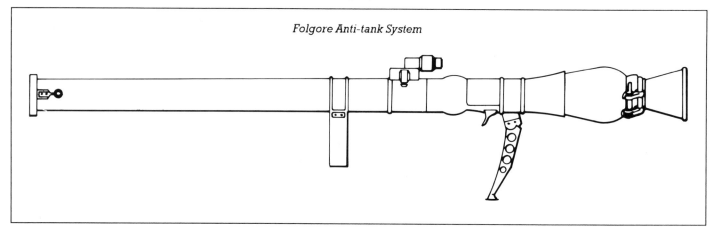

Folgore Anti-tank System

Specification:

Calibre: 80 mm

Weapon length: 1.80 m

Weapon weight: 18.0 kg

Projectile weight: 3 kg

Maximum range: 4500 m

Maximum velocity: 500 m/sec

Penetration of armour: >450 mm

Manufacturer: Breda Meccanica
Bresciana, Italy

Above Right: *The Italian Folgore anti-tank launcher with its optical sight.*

Below Right: *Folgore in the firing position with its two-man crew. The loader lies well clear of the back-blast and has the next round in his hand ready to reload. Empty cartridge cases lie behind the breech.*

APILAS Anti-tank Launcher South Africa

Apilas is the French equivalent of the British LAW 80, a one-man shoulder-fired anti-tank rocket which can be thrown away after use and which is capable of damaging the heaviest tanks. Developed by Manurhin Defense, a subsidiary of Giat Industries, the nationalised French munitions combine, **Apilas** has been adopted by France, Finland, Italy and several other countries as their primary infantry anti-armour weapon.

The **Apilas** launch tube is of spun aramid fibre and carries a retractable optical sight. Sealed inside is a rocket carrying a powerful shaped charge warhead which is electrically fuzed and armed by a gas-pressure generator which functions as the rocket is launched.

This system ensures that the rocket is completely safe until it is at least 10 metres from the launcher, and is completely armed and ready to function on impact by the time it is 25 metres away. The warhead has a long tapered nose cone which gives it the correct stand-off distance to penetrate over 700 mm of armour, and also allows the charge to function correctly at angles of oblique impact up to 80°.

In addition to its use against armour, **Apilas** is an effective anti-bunker weapon, capable of blowing quite large holes through more than two metres of reinforced concrete.

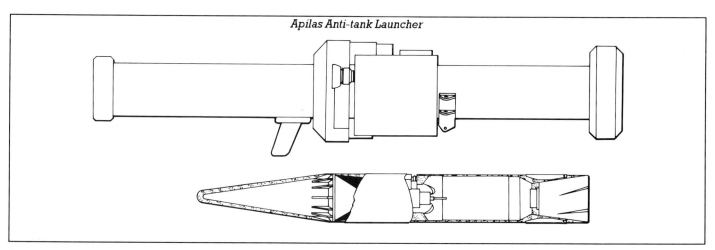

Apilas Anti-tank Launcher

Specification

Calibre of warhead: 112 mm

Weight in firing order: 9.0 kg

Length of launcher: 1290 mm

Maximum range: 330 m

Maximum velocity: 293 m/sec

Penetration of armour: >720 mm

Manufacturer: GIAT Industries, France

Aiming Apilas at an armoured target. Note that on this particular weapon the protective plastic foam end caps remain in place when firing.

SAM-7 STRELA AA Missile

F. Soviet Union

Development of this one-man missile system began in 1959 and first issues were made in 1966. It was used in the 1968/70 Egyptian-Israeli War and also in Vietnam.

Early versions were unreliable due to their infra-red seeker head being easily seduced off course by decoys, flares, the sun or even hot ground surfaces, but these defects were eventually cured and the final version was reasonably efficient. It is in wide use throughout the world, several countries making licensed copies.

Strela ('Arrow') consists of a grip-stock to which a thermal battery and a pre-packed missile in its launch tube can be quickly attached. The operator removes the front cover from the tube, exposing the infra-red seeker, points the assembly toward the target and acquires the target in his sight. He then pulls the two-stage trigger back to its first stop; this initiates the thermal battery and powers up the seeker and a stabilising gyroscope. The seeker detects the infra-red emissions from the target and once it has locked-on a green light appears in the sight and an audible signal informs the operator that he may fire. He presses the trigger back to the second stage and ignites a boost rocket which launches the missile from its tube. After leaving the tube the spent booster falls away and the main sustainer rocket ignites and accelerates the missile to its maximum speed. The seeker continues to track the target and steers the missile toward it by controlling two canard surfaces which spring out from the forward section of the missile.

The warhead is a simple high explosive charge in a fragmenting casing, with two impact fuzes, one acting on direct impact and the other reacting to a glancing blow should the missile not make a fair hit. If the missile fails to hit the target, it will self-destruct after 15 seconds or so of flight, which is about 6 km from the launcher.

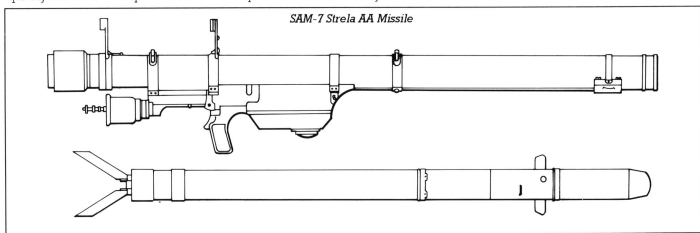

SAM-7 Strela AA Missile

Specification

Guidance: Infra-red seeker

Warhead diameter: 70 mm

Warhead weight: 1.15 kg

Launch unit weight: 10.6 kg

Missile weight: 9.2 kg

Missile length: 1300 mm

Max. effective range: 3500 m

Max. velocity: 385 m/sec

**Manufacturer: State Arsenals, Former
Soviet Union**

*The SAM-7 missile ready for use. The cylinder below the muzzle is the thermal
battery, providing power for starting the gyroscope and firing the boost rocket.
The foresight is behind the enlarged muzzle and the rearsight is above the trigger.*

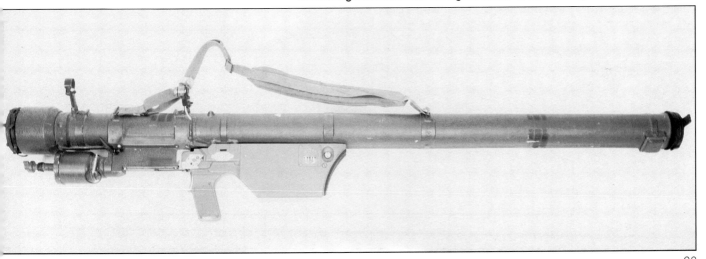

RPG-7 Anti-tank Launcher

The **RPG-7** first appeared in 1962, replacing the earlier RPG-2 which had its origin in the wartime German 'Panzerfaust'. The Panzerfaust was a hand-held recoilless gun, which limited the range, but the Russians improved on the original idea by adding a rocket to the actual projectile. This increased the range and also shortened the flight time, so making it slightly easier to hit moving targets.

The launcher is a 40 mm diameter tube with a convergent-divergent nozzle at the rear end. The tube is also fitted with a pistol grip, optical sight, shoulder rest, and a trigger connected to a simple percussion hammer. The projectile consists of a shaped charge explosive warhead, behind which is a solid-propellant rocket motor. Behind this is a thin tail boom carrying four fins which are folded forward like a knife-blade. A small propelling charge is fitted to the end of the rocket, and the projectile is loaded by pushing it into the front end of the tube, tail-first. A lug on the rocket fits into a notch in the barrel so as to align the ignition cap with the percussion hammer. The firer takes aim and presses the trigger to fire the propellant charge; this launches the projectile from the muzzle and ejects a blast of gas through the nozzle so that the launch effort is balanced and the weapon does not recoil. As the rocket leaves the tube, so the fins spring out to stabilise the flight, and after about 10 metres of flight the rocket ignites and accelerates the rocket to its full speed. This ignition point is very consistent and it is possible to place the rocket with some accuracy.

The tip of the warhead contains a piezo-electric crystal. When this strikes the target, the sudden compression of the crystal generates an electric current which is directed to a detonator at the base of the shaped charge. The charge detonates and develops a high speed, high temperature jet of molten metal and explosive gas which can pierce up to 330 mm of armour plate and do considerable damage after passing through the armour. Early versions used the metal of the warhead body as part of the electrical circuit and were thus easily short-circuited by hanging chicken-wire outside the target, but this defect was rapidly overcome and present-day fuzes are reliable.

The **RPG-7** is in wide use by former Warsaw Pact armies and many other forces around the world which have been supplied from Russia at various times. It is also manufactured in Egypt, Iraq, Pakistan and other countries.

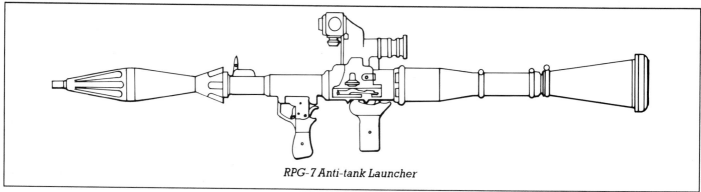

RPG-7 Anti-tank Launcher

Specification

Calibre of warhead: 85 mm

Weight in firing order: 10.15 kg

Length of launcher: 950 mm

Maximum range: 500 m stationary target;
300 m moving target

Maximum velocity: 300 m/sec

Penetration of armour: 330 mm

Manufacturer: State arsenals, Russia

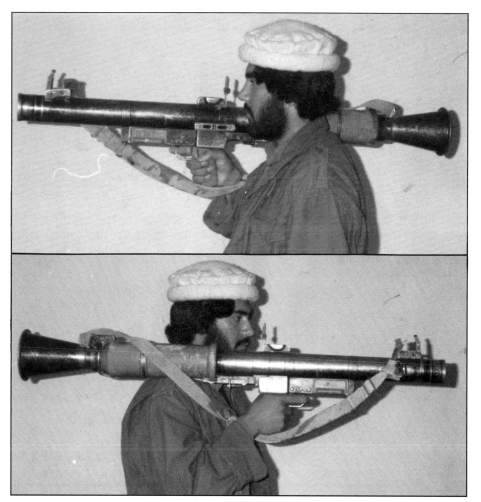

Above Right: Left side view of an Afghan Mujahedeen guerrilla taking aim with an empty RPG-7, and showing the sights and pistol grip.

Below Right: right side view of the Afghan and his RPG-7.

The **C90** began as a simple anti-tank rocket launcher, but it has since been upgraded and enhanced until it has become a multi-purpose weapon system which can be applied to various combat situations.

The basic weapon is a glass-fibre container-launcher, pre-loaded with a rocket carrying a shaped charge warhead. The container carries a sight, sling and a pistol grip and shoulder rest. The firing system is a simple percussion/pyrotechnic arrangement which means there is no requirement for batteries and thus no need for maintenance. The **C90** can be put on the shelf., pulled out and used at any time during a ten-year life. The optical sight has 2x magnification and a set of markings which indicate the aim-off necessary for moving targets of various speeds. It also has a permanent light source which illuminates the range markings in poor light.

The **C90-C** is the basic anti-tank weapon. The **C90-C-AM** has a different warhead on the rocket which incorporates a shaped charge and also a fragmentation sleeve around the charge so that as well as the anti-armour capability there is also a burst of about 1000 fragments covering a 20 metre radius around the point of impact, giving a very useful anti-personnel effect. The **C90-CR** has a much improved shaped charge warhead which can penetrate over 400 mm of armour (as opposed to the 250 mm or so of the original **C90**), while the **C90-CR-BK** uses a warhead containing a follow-through projectile. In this device, the shaped charge will blow a hole through the target's armour and then fire a small fragmenting grenade through the hole so as to burst inside the tank or pillbox and thus deal with the occupants.

And to demonstrate its total versatility there is the **C90-CR-FIM** which has a phosphorous-filled warhead capable of generating a screening smoke cloud or igniting any inflammable target. It is hardly surprising that in addition to being adopted by the Spanish Army, the **C90** has a healthy export market to several other armies.

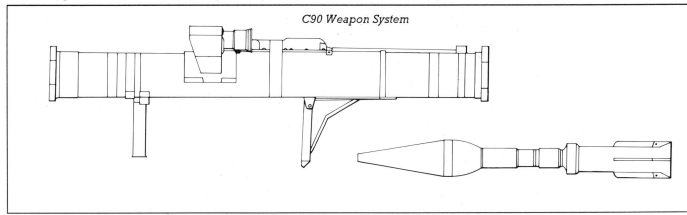

C90 Weapon System

Specification

Calibre of warhead: 90 mm

Weight in firing order: 4.2 kg

Length of launcher: 840 mm

Maximum range: 800 m

Anti-tank range: 200 m

Penetration of concrete: 1200 mm

Penetration of armour: 500 mm

Manufacturer: Instalaza SA, Spain

Firing the Spanish C-90 multi-purpose launcher in the anti-tank mode.

AT-4 Anti-tank Launcher Sweden

Bofors were early arrivals in the field of portable anti-tank weapons with their Carl Gustav gun (described elsewhere), and they also developed the 'Miniman', an early disposable launcher. But by building upon the technology of the Carl Gustav they have produced an effective and popular one-man launcher in their **AT-4** model. After adoption by the Swedish Army, **AT-4** was taken into service by the US Army and Navy, the Netherlands army, and several South American armies.

The **AT-4** is the usual sort of pre-packed shaped charge round inside a disposable sealed tube, but in this case the actual projectile is derived from the Carl Gustav gun shell, while the propulsion is based on the Carl Gustav cartridge, so that instead of the usual rocket, **AT-4** is a disposable recoilless gun. The pop-up sights are pre-calibrated for a range of 200 metres, although the rear sight can be adjusted to cater for wind or temperature, and the foresight has three marker posts to allow for aiming off against moving targets. The projectile is fin-stabilised, the fins springing out into the slipstream after leaving the muzzle, and the shaped charge warhead had been specially designed not only to punch through heavy armour but also to produce the maximum damage behind the armour from the flame and blast of the shaped charge jet.

AT-4 is also adaptable as an anti-bunker weapon. A special version, the **AT4 LMAW** (Light Multi-purpose Assault Weapon) has been developed using the special High Explosive Dual Purpose shell from Carl Gustav. This has a fuzing system which can be adjusted before firing to give either the full shaped charge anti-armour performance or a delay mode which allows the shell to be more effective against field fortifications, bunkers and similar targets.

A third variation, recently announced, is the **AT4CS**, the 'CS' standing for 'Confined Spaces'. This changes the propulsion and recoilless system to that of a countershot weapon, launching a mass of equal momentum rearwards as the projectile is launched forwards. This allows the weapon to be fired from inside rooms or other confined spaces without the backblast injuring the firer.

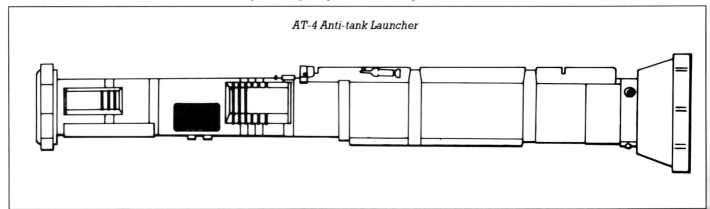

AT-4 Anti-tank Launcher

Specification

Calibre of warhead: 84 mm

Weight in firing order: 6.7 kg

Length of launcher: 1000 mm

Maximum range: 300 m

Maximum velocity: 290 m/sec

Penetration of armour: >400 mm

Manufacturer: Bofors Ordnance,
Sweden

Above Right: *AT-4 in the firing position, with sights erected.*

Below Right: *A cutaway view of AT-4 showing the rocket in its pre-packed position, sectioned to reveal the shaped charge liner and the rocket motor.*

CARL GUSTAV M2 84 mm Recoilless Gun　　Sweden

Carl Gustav was one of the first post-WW2 one-man anti-tank weapons, and by constant improvement has been among the leaders of this field ever since. It is in service with major armies around the world and is renowned for its versatility, having been used against armoured vehicles, field fortifications, helicopters and warships at various times.

The standard weapon is the Carl Gustav M2, an 84 mm breech-loading recoilless gun which can be fired from the shoulder. Although capable of being operated by one man, it is more usual to employ a two-man team, one holding and firing the gun while his partner stands to his rear and operates the breech to reload, a system which allows a rapid rate of fire. The ammunition consists of a complete round, a steel cartridge case holding the propelling charge and a shaped charge shell fitted into the mouth of the case. The base of the case is closed by a plastic disc, and on firing the pressure inside the cartridge case first starts the shell moving in the barrel and then ruptures the plastic disc and allows a quantity of high-velocity gas to be ejected through a venturi nozzle to the rear. The mass and velocity of the gas balances the mass and velocity of the shell so that there is no perceptible recoil felt by the firer.

An open sight is fitted, but the usual sight is a telescope which incorporates a temperature correction system and aids for aiming off against moving targets. Although the weapon is rifled, shaped charge performs best when not spinning, and the plastic sealing band around the shell is designed to slip and thus reduce the amount of spin on the shell; this is further reduced by pop-out fins which deploy after leaving the muzzle. In addition to the anti-armour projectile, smoke. illuminating and high explosive anti-personnel ammunition is also provided.

A lightweight version, the M3, is now manufactured, using a light high-strength steel barrel liner wrapped in a carbon-fibre laminate. This reduces the weight of the weapon to 8.5 kg without affecting performance and is likely to replace the earlier M2 model as these wear out.

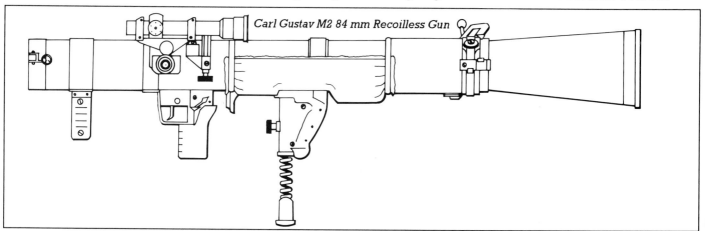

Carl Gustav M2 84 mm Recoilless Gun

Specification

Calibre of warhead: 84 mm

Weight in firing order: 14.2 kg

Length of launcher: 1130 mm

Maximum range: 700 m

Maximum velocity: 330 m/sec

Penetration of armour: >400 mm

Manufacturer: Bofors Ordnance,
        Sweden

*A British Grenadier Guardsman about to
fire Carl Gustav during exercises in Germany.
In this case the sprung supporting monopod
has been fitted close to the muzzle, a matter
of personal preference.*

RBS-70 AA MISSILE

Sweden

RBS-70 is a portable anti-aircraft missile system consisting of three units, sight, launching stand and missile, and can be placed in action in less than 30 seconds.

Guidance is based on an optical beam-riding system using a laser beam generated in the sight unit. The missile is pre-packed in a sealed container which is connected to the stand. The operator, alerted to the approach of a target by an observer, acquires the target in his sight, switches on the laser beam and prepares to fire the missile. An IFF (Identification, Friend or Foe) unit in the sight interrogates the target, and if it receives a signal indicating that the target is friendly it overrides the firing system and lights a lamp in the sight to inform the operator, who discontinues the action. If no IFF response is received, the missile is launched by a boost rocket, which burns out before leaving the launch tube. A few metres in front of the launcher the sustainer rocket motor ignites and the missile accelerates to supersonic speed. The missile is launched into the laser beam and a receiver in the tail picks up the beam and measures any difference between the missile's position and the axis of the beam, then makes the necessary corrections to fly the missile along the axis. All the operator now has to do is keep his sight aligned with the target, using a simple joystick control.

The missile is fitted with a shaped charge warhead which is encased in a pre-fragmented sleeve consisting of several hundred tungsten pellets. An impact fuze is fitted, and also a laser proximity fuze, so that a direct hit is not vital to success. On detonation, the shaped charge will penetrate any armour, while the tungsten pellets deliver a damaging cloud of fragments all round the point of detonation. The proximity fuze can be switched off if the target is close to the earth or some other reflecting surface - for example, a helicopter hovering over the tree-line; in this case the operator must obtain a direct hit in order to destroy the target.

The unit can also be connected to a 'Giraffe' search radar, which will then alert him to approaching targets and indicate their direction. He can then swing the launcher until an acoustic signal indicates he is correctly pointed for bearing; he then searches visually in elevation to acquire the target.

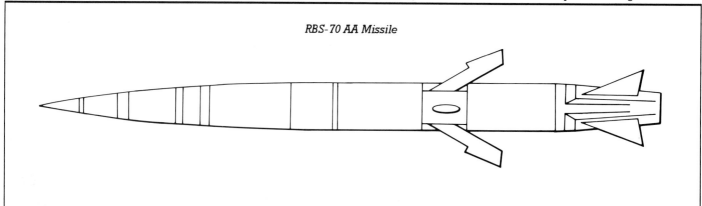

RBS-70 AA Missile

Specification

Guidance: Semi-automatic, laser beam-rider

Warhead diameter: 106 mm

Warhead weight: 1.0 kg

Launch unit weight: 57 kg

Missile weight: 16 kg

Missile length: 1320 mm

Max effective range: 7000 m

Max. velocity: Supersonic

Manufacturer: Bofors Missile Systems, Sweden

RBS-70 in the firing position. The laser beam projector is prominent in the front of the sighting and control unit. This system was originally known as the "Ray-Rider".

BLOWPIPE AA Missile

Blowpipe was the first shoulder-fired AA missile to be employed by the British Army and is still in use by several countries. It saw service in the Falklands campaign of 1982 but has been replaced in British service by the Javelin, an improved model. It remains in limited production for export orders. **Blowpipe** differs from other air defence missiles in being completely controlled during flight by the operator, rather than relying upon infra-red homing, making it an outstanding weapon for frontal attack of aircraft before they are in bombing range.

Blowpipe consists of two basic units, the sight unit and the missile in its sealed storage and launch container. The two are clipped together and the operator places it on his shoulder and takes aim through the optical sight. The handgrip has a firing trigger and a thumb-operated flight controller. Pulling the trigger energises the thermal battery to provide power for the aiming unit and the missile and then fires the boost rocket which ejects the missile from the launch tube; a few yards from the tube, the sustainer motor ignites and the missile accelerates to maximum speed. Four fins spring out as the missile is launched, and control surfaces on the nose section control the steering of the missile. Flares at the rear are tracked by a receiver in the sight and corrections to bring the missile into the sight axis are generated and transmitted so as to gather the missile into the line of sight. Thereafter, steering is controlled by the operator, using his thumb control to keep the missile on its correct course. If the missile is accurately guided and hits the target, then an impact fuze detonates the warhead. If it is a near miss, the proximity fuze detects the presence of the target and determines when the missile is within lethal range, whereupon it detonates the fragmentation warhead.

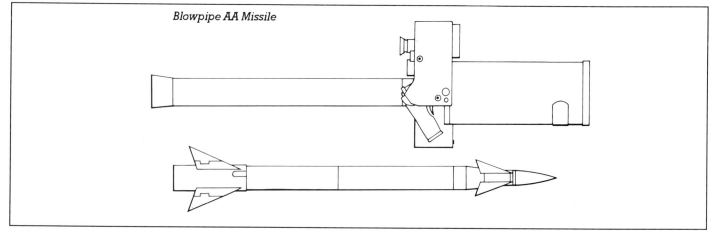

Blowpipe AA Missile

Specification

Guidance: Manual guidance, radio command

Warhead diameter: 76 mm

Warhead weight: 2.20 kg

Launch unit weight: 6.2 kg

Missile weight: 11 kg

Missile length: 1350 mm

Max. effective range: 3500 m

Minimum effective range: 700 m

Max. velocity: Mach 1

Manufacturer: Short Brothers, UK

Above Right: A close-up of the Blowpipe control unit showing how the operator controls the missile's flight by using his thumb.

Below Right: About to fire Blowpipe; the operator is tracking the target and interrogating the IFF system before pressing the firing switch.

LAW 80 Anti-tank Launcher

Whilst the M66 is an effective weapon against the lighter types of armoured vehicle, it lacks the necessary punch to be able to threaten main battle tanks. As a result, several countries have developed heavier shoulder-fired launchers for this task, and the current British weapon is the **LAW 80**.

LAW 80 is a one-shot disposable weapon which can engage heavy armoured targets out to ranges of up to 500 metres. It consists of a telescoping tubular launcher pre-packer with a shaped charge rocket, and the unit also includes a spotting rifle firing a special bullet which matches the trajectory of the rocket and provides a visible flash and puff of smoke on impact. The soldier prepares the launcher by removing the protective end caps and extending the rear tube, which contains the rocket. He then places the weapon on his shoulder, takes aim through the small optical sight, and presses the trigger to fire the spotting rifle. The rifle is a self-loader and carries five rounds in its magazine, so that up to five aiming shots can be fired. Once the soldier sees a shot strike the target he presses forward the change lever with his thumb and, maintaining the same point of aim, pressed the trigger to fire the rocket. The rocket motor burns out before the rocket has left the launcher, thus ensuring that the backblast is confined by the tube and directed well behind the firer.

The warhead is fitted with a piezo-electric fuzing system and various safe-and-arm devices which ensure that the warhead is not armed until the rocket is well clear of the launcher. On impact, an electrical impulse fires a detonator at the rear of the shaped charge which then develops the usual jet of high temperature gas and molten metal to penetrate over 700 mm of armour plate.

LAW 80 is a versatile weapon; in addition to its normal shoulder-fired role it can be positioned on a ground mount and used as a 'stand-off' anti-tank mine, either fired by electrical command, by an autonomous sensor which detects the presence of a tank or by a timing device

LAW 80 Anti-tank Launcher

Specification

Calibre of warhead: 94 mm

Weight in firing order: 9.0 kg

Length of launcher: 1500 mm

Maximum range: 500 m

Penetration of armour: 700 mm

Manufacturer: Hunting Engineering, UK

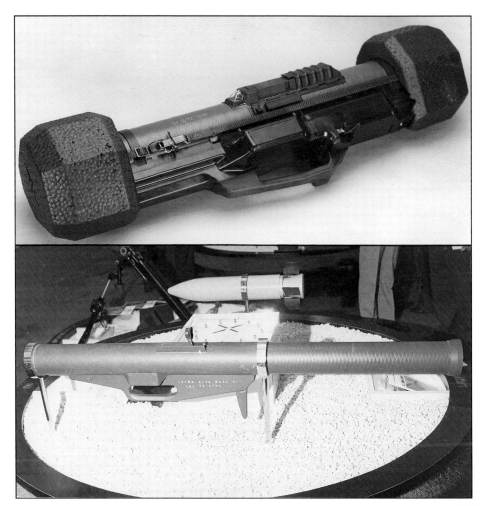

Above Right: an early example of the LAW 80 anti-tank launcher in the fully extended position, together with its rocket.

Below Right: The production LAW 80 with its protective end caps in place and the sight folded. The rectangular plate above the hand grip is the magazine for the incorporated aiming rifle.

M72 66 mm Anti-tank Launcher USA

One of the first 'disposable' weapons to be used in quantity, the **M72 LAW** (Light Anti-armour Weapon) was developed in the 1960s in the USA and was a revolutionary idea: a pre-packed rocket which could be fired and the launcher then thrown away. Light, compact, easily carried, it was destructive not only of armour but also of field fortifications, pill-boxes and similar hard targets. It was widely adopted throughout NATO and in many other countries and has since been copied on both sides of the Iron Curtain.

The **M72** consists of a telescoping launch tube, the inner tube being of aluminium and the outer of glass-fibre. This carries a simple sight and a firing mechanism. As issued, the tubes are telescoped together and inside is a shaped-charge rocket unit with a solid-propellant motor. The ends are sealed by metal caps and a sling allows the soldier to carry the complete unit over his shoulder. When required, he simply casts off the end caps and extends the tube. This automatically cocks the firing mechanism and erects the sight. Placing the tube on his shoulder, the man takes aim and squeezes the trigger. This ignites the rocket, which is launched from the tube, and the man then simply throws the tube away.

The current version of the **M72** is known as the 'Improved E Series' and has a number of improvements over the earlier models. The sight is improved, the rocket motor is more powerful, and thus the effective range has been increased from 170 to 220 metres, while the hit probability has been doubled.

The **M72** is manufactured in the USA and also in Norway for supply to NATO forces. It has been copied, in principle, in both Czechoslovakia and Russia as the RPG-18 and RPG-26, both of somewhat larger calibre than the **M72** but of about the same tactical performance.

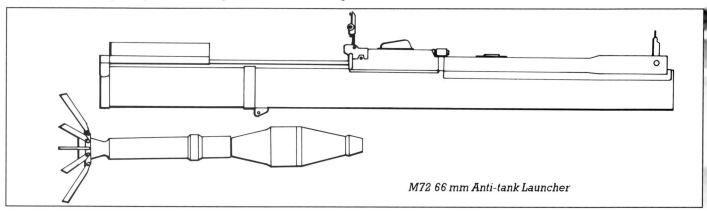

M72 66 mm Anti-tank Launcher

Specification

Calibre of warhead: 66 mm

Weight in firing order: 3.45 kg

Length of launcher: 980 mm

Maximum range: 220 m

Maximum velocity: 200 m/sec

Penetration of armour: 350 mm

Manufacturer: Talley Industries, USA

The M72 66 mm anti-tank launcher extended and about to be fired. The soldier's left hand supports the launcher, while the fingers of his right hand are on the trigger on top of the launcher.

STINGER AA Missile USA

Stinger is a shoulder-fired missile which is an improved version of the US Army's original 'Redeye' missile. It has more range, can engage any aspect of the target, has improved manoeuverability and is much more resistant to countermeasures, decoys and other non-target sources of infra-red energy.

The missile is pre-packed in a transport and launch tube and is clipped on to a separate grip-stock which carries the firing mechanism, sight, IFF antenna and system electronics. The tube is discarded after each firing and a fresh missile and tube attached.

The missile carries an infra-red seeker unit in the nose, electronic guidance circuits, a high explosive/fragmentation warhead with impact fuze, and a dual-thrust solid-fuel rocket motor. The seeker is a very advanced dual-frequency device which is sensitive to both infra-red and ultra-violet light and can discriminate between genuine and spurious target indications.

The firing sequence is relatively simple; with the two units assembled, the operator unfolds the IFF antenna and removes the front cap from the launch tube to expose the IR seeker head of the missile. He unfolds the sight and takes aim at the target, triggering the IFF system as he does so. If no response is heard, then the target is assumed enemy; he then activates the weapon system, switching on the seeker and running up the stabilising gyroscope. Once the seeker has identified and locked on to the target, an audible signal is given and the operator can unlock the missile gyroscope and press the trigger. This fires the boost rocket which throws the missile out of the tube, the control surfaces and stabilising fins springing out as it leaves. A few metres away from the tube the sustainer rocket motor ignites and the missile flies off towards the target. The operator can now throw away the spent tube and reload; his part in the operation is over and the missile will now track the target, steer itself to impact and detonate. Should some failure cause it to miss, then a self-destruction device will detonate it some 6 km from launch.

As well as its use as a man-portable system, **Stinger** has also been adapted as a helicopter-borne system, and several proposals for vehicle mounts, in conjunction with 25mm cannon, have been put forward. A night sight has also been developed, using a third-generation image intensifying system; a limited number of these were procured by the US Marine Corps and were used with some success during Operation Desert Storm.

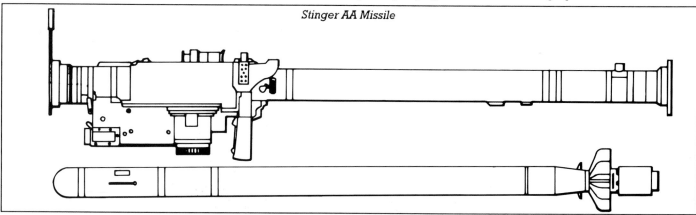

Stinger AA Missile

Specification

Guidance: Infra-red homing

Warhead diameter: 70 mm

Warhead weight: 3 kg

Launch unit weight: 15.7 kg

Missile weight: 10.1 kg

Missile length: 1524 mm

Max effective range: >4500 m

Max velocity: Mach 2.2

Manufacturer: General Dynamics, USA

Stinger in the firing position. The vertically-slotted plate is part of the IFF system. The box at the rear end and the sight are both experimental units which were not brought into service.

SMAW (Shoulder-launched Multi-purpose Assault Weapon) has been designed to answer two requirements, the first for a shoulder-fired anti-tank weapon and the second for a similar anti-hard target weapon. In the past anti-tank rockets have been used to attack bunkers and field fortifications, but although they make a hole, it is not a particularly large one and the effect behind the protection is limited. By providing specially-designed rounds for the two distinctly different tasks, **SMAW** can be easily switched from one task to the other.

The launcher itself is a simple tube with a firing mechanism and a sight. The round of ammunition is pre-packed into a sealed tube which is attached to the rear end of the launcher tube by a quick bayonet joint. Attaching the tube automatically links up the firing system, and all the user has to do is take aim and pull the trigger. An ejection charge shoots the projectile from the launcher, after which the rocket ignites and the projectile is accelerated to the target. The empty firing tube is removed from the launcher and discarded, and a new tube attached.

For dealing with armour, the prepacked round carries a shaped charge warhead which can defeat 600 mm of homogenous rolled steel armour at an impact angle of 70°. This projectile can be used to engage tank-sized targets out to 500 metres range.

For dealing with field fortifications, the prepacked round uses the HE Dual Purpose warhead; this has a unique fuzing system which ensures that if the target is hard, then the detonation occurs on its surface, whilst if the target is soft the warhead is allowed to penetrate some distance before the detonation so as to do the maximum amount of damage to the structure.

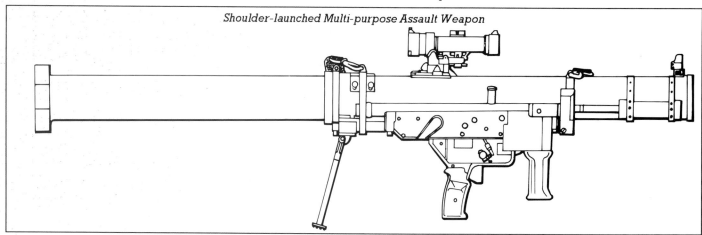

Shoulder-launched Multi-purpose Assault Weapon

Specification

Calibre of warhead: 83 mm

Weight in firing order: 13.4 kg

Length of launcher: 825 mm

Maximum range: 500 m

Maximum velocity: 220 m/sec

Penetration of armour: >600 mm

Manufacturer: McDonnell Douglas, USA

Firing SMAW at a bunker. The actual weapon is only the front half of the assembly on the man's shoulder, the rear half being the pre-packed rocket and container which is only attached to the weapon immediately before firing.

AT-8 Bunker Buster

USA

The US Army adopted the AT-4 anti-tank launcher (described previously) as their M136 in 1990, and after some experience with it decided that a similar weapon optimised for use against bunkers and field fortifications would be an advantage. The AT-4 was being made in the USA, under licence from Bofors, by Alliant TechSystems, and they set about changing the design to meet the US Army's requirement.

The resulting weapon is the **AT-8**, a light, disposable weapon capable of breaching walls, destroying fortified targets and, in emergency, defending against attacks by light armoured vehicles such as Infantry Fighting Vehicles and reconnaissance tanks.

The weapon takes the existing AT-4 disposable tube launcher and pre-loads it with a projectile developed in conjunction with the US Marine Corps. The warhead is a somewhat modified shaped charge, allied with a dual fuzing system which distinguishes between hard and soft targets. Against a hard target the fuze acts instantly and detonates the charge at the optimum point outside the target so as to develop the nest penetrative effect. However, the shaped charge is designed to deliver a much thicker jet of explosive gas against the target than that produced by a 'pure' anti-tank charge, so that the hole in the target is quite large and the behind-protection effect considerable. If the target is soft, then the fuze delays its action for a few microseconds

to allow the warhead to get well into the structure of the target or, in the case of a thin-walled target, pass completely through and into the protected space. It then detonates, and if it is within the structure there will be considerable rupture and breaching, while if it has passed through there will be the maximum effect on the personnel and equipment behind the protection.

Since the **AT-8** uses exactly the same launcher as the AT-4, there is no problem in re-training the soldier; if he has been trained on AT-4 he can just as easily use **AT-8**. Moreover the launcher has been designed with an integral mount which will accept various night vision devices, so permitting accurate fire in conditions of darkness.

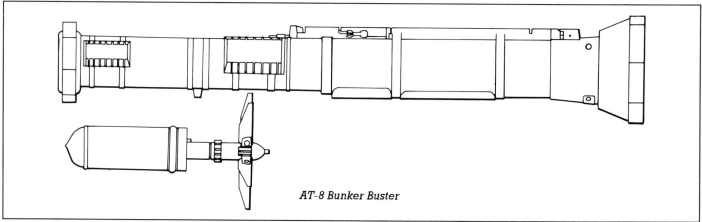

AT-8 Bunker Buster

Specification

Calibre of warhead: 84 mm

Weight in firing order: 7.17 kg

Length of launcher: 1000 mm

Maximum range: 250 m

Maximum velocity: 219 m/sec

Manufacturer: Alliant TechSystems, USA

Preparing to fire the AT-8. The firer's fingers are on the trigger and the sight erected. The frangible seal in front of the launch tube can also be seen.

SUPERDRAGON Anti-tank Missile   USA

The Dragon anti-tank missile was adopted by the US Army in the early 1970s as a one-man, shoulder-fired short range guided missile. It uses an unusual propulsion and guidance system; the rocket has a rear boost motor which launches it from its storage tube, after which 30 pairs of side thrusting solid fuel rocket are brought into play as required. These small rockets are set into the body of the missile, pointing outwards and rearwards so that when they are ignited the give both rearward thrust to propel the missile and side thrust to steer it. Ignition of these rockets is controlled by the computer built into the sight unit. The firer launches the missile and keeps his sight lined up with the target; the sight detects an infra-red flare in the tail of the missile, determines its offset from the sight line, and then fires a combination of rockets to deliver the necessary forward thrust to sustain its speed and side thrust to steer it in the desired direction. The missile position is constantly monitored and rockets are being fired in various combinations throughout the flight so as to keep the missile on the line of sight.

Dragon I entered service in 1970 and had a range of 1000 metres which it covered in 11 seconds. Dragon II appeared about ten years later and had an improved warhead which gave much greater penetration of armour. Dragon III, which later evolved into the present **Superdragon**, was developed in 1989-90 and uses a further improved warhead, this having an extensible probe with tandem shaped charges to defeat explosive reactive armour and an additional sustainer motor to provide more of the forward propulsion and thus shorten the flight time as well as extending the range; it can now fly to 1500 metres in 8.6 seconds.

Superdragon is delivered to the user as a pre-packed missile in a launch and storage tube which carries a small bipod. The firer clamps on the sight and tracking unit, extends the bipod to the required height, and kneels, supporting the rear end of the ;launch tube on his shoulder. After firing he maintains his aim until the missile impacts, then detaches the sight unit and throws the tube away. **Superdragon** is also supplied with a new day/night tracker unit which uses infra-red vision for night firing.

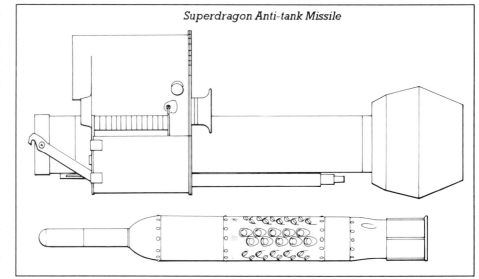

Superdragon Anti-tank Missile

Specification

Guidance: Semi-automatic, wire

Warhead diameter: ca 140 mm

Launch unit weight: 6.9 kg

Missile weight: 10.07 kg

Missile length: 852 mm

Max. effective range: 1500 m

Max. velocity: ca 200 m/sec

Penetration of armour: >500 mm

Manufacturer: McDonnell Douglas
Aerospace, USA

Dragon in the firing position. The unusual front support allows the firer to kneel and thus obtain a better viewpoint, and it also ensures that the control wire is less likely to snag on battlefield debris lying on the ground.

TOW 2 Anti-tank Missile

TOW (Tube-launched, Optically-tracked, Wire-guided) began in 1962 and the missile went into service with the US Army in 1970. It has been used in combat in Vietnam and in the Middle East and has been adopted by some 17 countries in various parts of the world. Over some 12,000 firings since 1970 has enabled the US Army to establish that it is 93 percent reliable. It is used on ground, vehicle or helicopter mountings.

The **TOW M220A1** weapon system comprises six main units: tripod, traversing unit, launch tube, optical sight, guidance set and battery assembly. The traversing unit sits on the tripod and carries the optical sight and guidance set. The launch tube, with a pre-packed missile, clips on to the traversing unit. To engage a target the firer takes aim and presses the trigger. This launches the missile from its tube by using a boost motor, after which the sustainer motor ignites about 12 metres in front of the launcher. Two control wires are laid from the rear of the missile as it flies, and these are used to pass steering messages from the guidance unit to the missile. The system is the usual SACLOS system, a flare in the tail located by a sensor in the sight which then determines the spatial difference between the missile and the line of sight and generates the corrections to fly the missile into alignment with the target.

TOW has been subject to a continuous improvement programme during its life, directed both at the warhead and at the control system. The first warhead was 127 mm diameter, and this was improved by the addition of an extended fuze probe to give a more consistent stand-off distance which improved the penetration. The next upgrade (**TOW 2**) was to a 152 mm warhead, improved guidance circuits and a more powerful sustainer motor. **TOW 2A** added a small shaped precursor charge to the fuze probe so as to detonate explosive reactive armour, while **TOW 2B** adopted a top-attack warhead containing two shaped charges which point obliquely down so as to attack the thinner upper surfaces of the tank. Work is currently proceeding on **FITOW** (Further Improved TOW) in which a proximity fuze and top attack warhead will be used.

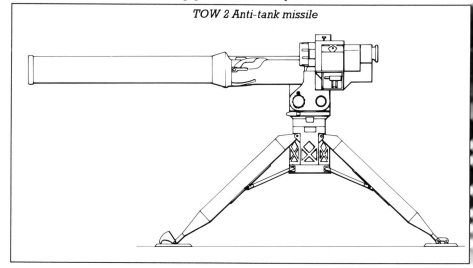

TOW 2 Anti-tank missile

Specification

Guidance: Semi-automatic, wire

Warhead diameter: 127 mm

Launch unit weight: 87.5 kg

Missile weight: 28 kg

Missile length: 1174 mm

Max. effective range: 3750 m

Max. velocity: 200 m/sec

Penetration of armour: >700mm

**Manufacturer: Hughes Missile Systems,
USA**

*A team from the Combat Support Company,
5th US Infantry Regiment, tracking a target
with TOW, using the original optical day sight.
More recent versions use an improved sight
with day and night capability.*

JAVELIN AAWS/M

The drawback to wire-guided missiles is that the operator has to maintain his aim to the target for the whole duration of the missile's flight; this may be no more than 10 or 12 seconds, but it still takes a great deal of skill and courage to concentrate upon a distant target in the stress of battle, and a too-close burst of machine gun fire can often put the operator off his target long enough for the missile to go astray. Therefore, the ambition of designers has been to develop a 'fire and forget' missile, one which the operator can forget as soon as he has launched it and can either take cover or look for another target.

Javelin AAWS/M (Anti-Armor Weapon System, Medium) is to be the US Army's fire-and-forget missile. It consists of two

units, the Command Launch Unit (CLU) which is the sight and firing system, and the missile itself, pre-packed in the usual type of sealed container. The two units are quickly connected together, the assembly placed on the shoulder and fired, the empty tube discarded and a fresh tube fitted.

The missile uses an infra-red seeker head which is programmed to recognise the typical shape and signature of a tank and to ignore other heat sources. When aiming the weapon, the seeker is lined up with the target and once it 'recognises' what it sees, it is fired. A boost rocket launches it from the tube, after which a sustainer rocket ignites and accelerates the missile down-range. Once locked on to the target

the missile will continue to track it, ignoring distractions such as heat decoys or other tanks. It is flight-programmed to fly somewhat higher than the initial sight line, and the powerful shaped charge warhead is canted downwards so that as the missile flies over the tank, the charge fires down and penetrates the more vulnerable upper surfaces of the target. Conventional missiles attack the sides of the tank, where the armour is thickest; top attack allows a slightly smaller warhead to be used, giving the missile higher speed and longer range.

Development of this missile has been in progress since the early 1980s, and it is anticipated that it should reach the hands of troops in 1996.

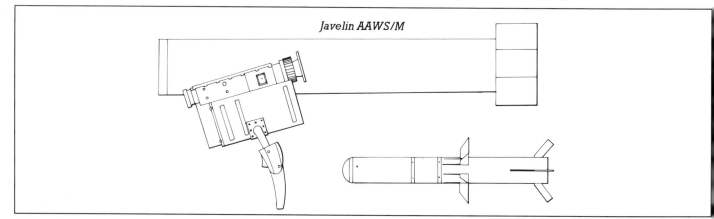

Javelin AAWS/M

Specification

Calibre of warhead: 127 mm

Weight in firing order: 15.88 kg

Length of launcher: 1000 mm

Maximum range: 2000 m

Maximum velocity: 290 m/sec

Penetration of armour: >400 mm

Manufacturer: Texas Instruments/Martin
Marietta, USA

Firing the Javelin AAWS/M anti-armour missile. Since it is a fire-and-forget system there is no need to have a tripod mount since there is no control wire to require anchoring.

Surveillance Equipment

At first glance a battle field is an empty place, because soldiers are well aware that being conspicuous is hazardous to your health. Therefore it becomes necessary to hunt for targets. You could use a weapon sight, but this means either swinging the weapon around or removing the sight, with all the risk of having to put it back in a hurry if trouble arises. Moreover, instruments designed as sights are not necessarily well-adapted for searching. And so a whole range of target-seeking and front-observing devices has appeared in the past twenty or so years. As might be expected, they include a wide selection of powerful night vision devices capable of locating targets several miles away, with pinpoint accuracy. But they also include such things as short range radar sets capable of detecting anything from a crawling man to a squadron of tanks and positively identifying them, measuring their speed and plotting their course. Acoustic detectors can be buried which will detect any sound and analyse it, from a footstep to a tank track, and automatically relay the information by radio to whoever requires it. As a result, the battlefield no longer closes down as darkness falls; it is alive and under close surveillance for 24 hours of every day. The only remaining question is when do the soldiers find time to sleep?

Another long range observation device, the American Baird GP/NVB-6A is for use in front-line sentry posts in order to keep a check on the front during darkness.

Below: Although originally intended for use by vehicle drivers, night vision goggles are also useful for sentries and night patrols. A pair of these, plus a laser spot projector on the man's weapon, and you have a virtually foolproof method of night fighting.

Below: The all-singing stereo solution. This combination instrument has a laser rangefinder, gyro-compass, optical sight and micro-processor built-in. It can be linked by line or radio to a rear command centre and it will instantly determine the coordinates of whatever targets it is directed towards.

Above: *Surveillance and retaliation. This unit carries a video camera, spotlights and two machine guns. For use in guarding fixed installations, it is connected to a control computer. As it continuously scans its allotted zone, any movement or change in the picture stored in memory will cause it to swing on to the target and alert the operator. He can challenge the intruder by means of a loud hailer, and if he gets the wrong answer can open fire with the machine guns.*

TARASQUE 20 mm AA Gun — France

Tarasque is a single-barrel, power-operated, towed anti-aircraft gun fitted with a 20 mm F2 cannon. Although primarily designed for use against aircraft it is also a useful ground support weapon, able to deliver a stream of highly damaging explosive shells against field fortifications and similar targets.

Towed on a two-wheeled trailer by any light vehicle, **Tarasque** can be placed in action with wheels removed in about 15 seconds. Power is provided by a petrol engine driving a hydraulic motor to pressurise a system which then operates the traverse and elevation mechanisms and also cocks the gun. Should the motor fail, it is possible to hand-pump the hydraulic reservoir up to pressure, after which the gun can be cocked and the mounting operated for sufficient time for the average anti-aircraft engagement.

A seat is provided for the gunner, who has a foot-pedal trigger and manual safety and ammunition controls. Emergency hand-operated controls for elevation and traverse are provided. The sight is a dual-purpose design, with a 1x telescope for aerial targets and a 5x telescope for ground targets.

The gun is fed by two belts, one on each side, and either belt can be switched into the feed system as required. This allows two types of ammunition to be available for use; one belt can be filled with anti-aircraft explosive ammunition, while the other can have armour-piercing ammunition in readiness for ground targets. Normally, one belt carries 90 rounds of HE and the other 40 rounds of armour-piercing discarding sabot ammunition. The armour-piercing shot is capable of defeating 20 mm of armour at 1000 metres range. The gun can be fired in the single shot mode or in automatic mode.

The normal crew is three men; the gunner on the gun and one man on either side attending to the ammunition replenishment. As well as being used on this field mount, the basic gun carriage can be mounted on the cargo bed of a two-tonne truck. It has been in service with the French Army since 1982 and has also been sold to some Central African countries.

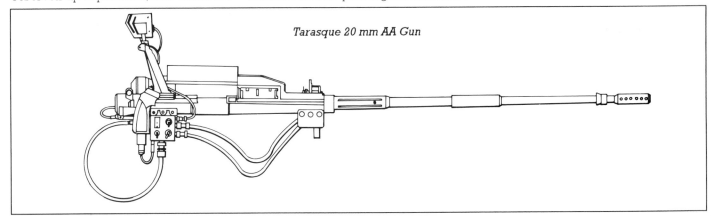

Tarasque 20 mm AA Gun

Specification

Cartridge: 20 x 139 mm

Operating system: Delayed blowback

Weight, empty: 70 kg gun; 650 kg
complete equipment

Length overall: 2207 mm gun;

Barrel: 2065 mm

Feed system: Dual disintegrating link belt

Rate of Fire: 900 rounds/min

Effective range: 2000 m

Muzzle velocity: 1050 m/sec

Manufacturer: GIAT Industries, France

The 20 mm Tarasque in action. The gunner's seat and sight unit move bodily with the gun in elevation, so that there is no need to design a complicated mechanism to move the sight line of a stationary sight.

ZPU 14.5 mm AA Machine Gun · F. Soviet Union

The **ZPU** anti-aircraft equipments are all armed with the Vladimirov KPV machine gun, a heavy weapon which was developed in the late 1940s to take advantage of the powerful 14.5 mm cartridge which had been developed during the war for use in an anti-tank rifle. The gun was designed primarily as an anti-aircraft weapon and was first issued in the late 1940s as the **ZPU-1**, a two-wheeled trailer with a single gun. Shortly afterwards the **ZPU-2** appeared, a somewhat more robust trailer mounting two guns on a turntable and fitted with a tachymetric sight into which the course and estimated speed of the target could be set and which then indicated the amount and direction necessary to aim off.

The first **ZPU-2** had the wheels removed when being brought into action and then sat on a three-legged platform. A later version was somewhat lighter and the wheels were simply raised so as to drop the platform to the ground.

Whilst this was an effective weapon, the increasing speed of aircraft made it necessary to increase the amount of metal thrown into the air in the brief time the target was in range, and in 1949 the **ZPU-4** appeared. This used a large four-wheeled carriage, upon which was a turntable with a mounting holding four guns

and their ammunition feed boxes, together with an advanced optical computing sight. The equipment could be put into action in less than half a minute, the wheels being raised and two outriggers swung out on either side. Screw jacks at the ends of the carriage and outriggers allowed the mounting to be levelled. In an emergency it was possible to fire the guns while the mounting was still in the travelling position, supported on its wheels, but due to the tyres and suspension moving under the firing

impulse, accuracy suffered.

In addition to these towed mounts, the 2-barrel version was also fitted into the chassis of various personnel carriers to acts as a self-propelled gun for convoy protection. All models of the **ZPU** were used by the Soviet and other Warsaw Pact armies and large numbers were supplied to foreign countries, notably in Africa, the Middle and Far East and South America. Numbers of **ZPU-4** were also manufactured in China and North Korea.

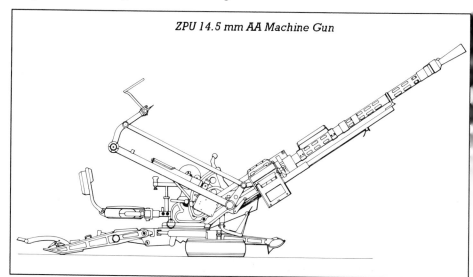

ZPU 14.5 mm AA Machine Gun

Specifications:

Cartridge: 14.5 x 114 mm Soviet

Operating system: Recoil, with gas assistance

Weight, empty: 49 kg (gun);

Length overall: 2006 mm (gun)

Barrel: 1346 mm, 8 grooves, rh

Feed system: Disintegrating link belt

Rate of Fire: 600 rounds/min

Muzzle velocity: 1000 m/sec

Manufacturer: State Arsenals,
F. Soviet Union

The 14.5 m ZPU-4, four barrelled anti-aircraft equipment at practice in Siberian snow in the 1970s.

ZU 23 mm AA Cannon

The **ZU-23** series of weapons greatly resembles the ZPU 14.5 mm series described above, and was developed in the early 1960s in order to replace those machine guns with a more destructive weapon capable of inflicting damage on modern armoured aircraft. The cannon solution also allowed the use of high explosive projectiles, capable of doing far more damage than the same weight of solid bullets fired from a machine gun. A ready method of identifying the two equipments lies in the flash hiders on the gun muzzles and the ammunition supply boxes alongside the guns. In the 14.5 mm ZPU equipment the flash hiders are conical and the ammunition boxes vertical; in the **ZU-23** the flash hiders are tubular and the ammunition boxes horizontal.

The **ZU-23** cannon is gas operated and uses a vertical sliding breech block. It can feed its belt from either side by a simple adjustment, and fires a bottle-necked cartridge with high explosive or HE/Incendiary shells fitted with impact fuzes. The barrels are fitted with carrying handles which allow them to be quickly removed and replaced when overheated from long firing.

The mounting is a two-wheeled trailer of triangular shape. To place it in action the two wheels are raised and the platform lowered to the ground. Three screw jacks at the corners are then operated to level the platform. All operation is manual, and a tachymetric sight, which compensates for target course and speed, is fitted. There is no provision for the receipt of data from predictors or other fire control systems, and thus the **ZU-23** must be classed as a 'fair weather system', only capable of operation when the target is optically visible to the gunners.

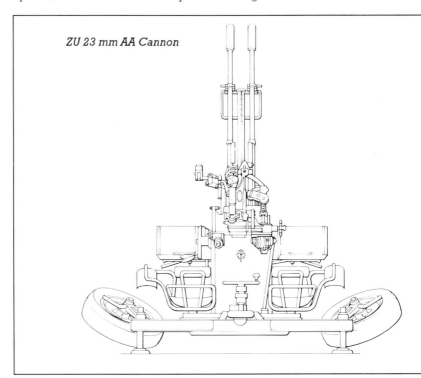

ZU 23 mm AA Cannon

Specification

Cartridge: 23 x 152 mm

Operating system: Gas, automatic

Weight, empty: 75 kg gun

Length overall: 2555 mm gun;

Barrel: 2010 mm, 10 grooves, rh, increasing twist

Feed system: Disintegrating link belt

Rate of Fire: 800 - 1000 rounds/min per gun

Muzzle velocity: 970 m/sec

Manufacturer: State arsenals, F. Soviet Union

A twin-gun ZPU-23 equipment about to open fire at a ground target, while the spare members of the crew take up defensive positions.

DIANA 25 mm AA Cannon

Switzerland

The equipment known as 'Diana' is a trailer-mounted twin 25 mm cannon with auxiliary propulsion, and is a good example of modern air defence technology.

The unit consists of an armoured gunner's cabin with sighting system and power supply installation. Alongside the cab are the two guns, and between them, behind the cab, is the ammunition magazine. Cabin and guns are mounted on a two-wheeled trailer; to emplace, the wheels are removed, outriggers extended and the platform levelled by hand jacks. In an emergency the wheels can be lowered and the power supply motor can then be geared into the side wheels and a third dolly wheel lowered, so that the entire mounting can be driven for short distances when the normal towing vehicle is not available. Steering is controlled by varying the speed of the hydraulic motors in each wheel.

The unit is provided as standard with a computing optical sight, but could also be fitted with a Contraves 'Gun King' sight which incorporates a laser rangefinder and an electronic computer which compensates for all ballistic variables, calculates the aim-off for target movement and other variables and re-sets the sight graticule accordingly.

While this weapon is completely autonomous, it can, if desired, by linked into most forms of radar fire control system so that the gunner can be directed by data link towards an approaching target and then engage it using his own sights once it is within range.

Two versions of Diana exist; the first used the 25 mm KBA cannon, firing the 25 x 137 mm cartridge and with the data given in the table. The other uses the KBB cannon, firing the more powerful 25 x 184 mm cartridge and with a somewhat higher muzzle velocity.

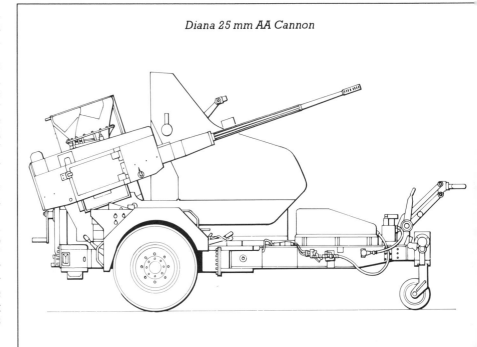

Diana 25 mm AA Cannon

Specification

Cartridge: 25 x 137 mm NATO

Operating system: Gas, selective fire

Weight, empty: 112 kg (gun);
2100 kg (complete equipment)

Length overall: 2888 mm (gun)

Barrel: 2173 mm, 18 grooves, rh,
increasing twist

Feed system: Dual belts, selective, instant
changeover

Rate of Fire: 600 rounds/min per gun

Muzzle velocity: 1100 - 1375 m/sec

Manufacturer: Oerlikon-Contraves,
Switzerland

Front view of the Diana anti-aircraft system, showing the electro-optical computing sight in front of the gunner and the side-mounted cannon.

Rear view of the Diana system, showing the magazine behind the gunner's cabin and the belt feed to one of the two cannon.

M242 Chain Gun

The Chain Gun is a mechanically actuated machine gun which takes its name from, the endless chain which is at the heart of the mechanism. It was originally developed by Hughes Helicopters, and some 10,000 Chain Guns of various calibres have been delivered since production began in 1981. In 7.62 mm calibre it is fitted to the British Army's 'Warrior' infantry fighting vehicle. This 25 mm version is found on the US Army's 'Bradley' infantry fighting vehicle, the US Marine LAV-25 light armoured vehicle, and on deck mountings on US Naval patrol boats.

The Chain Gun is powered by an electric motor. This drives a gear-wheel which is engaged with an endless loop of chain which lies in the bottom of the gun's receiver.

One link of this chain is engaged with the bolt carrier of the gun, so that as the chain is driven by the motor, the link moves forward along one side of the receiver, across the front behind the breech, back down the other side, across the back, and then forward again to repeat the cycle. Thus the bolt carrier is driven forward on the forward movement, remains closed up against the breech as the link crosses the front, is withdrawn as the link goes back, and again remains stationary as the link crosses the back end. The bolt fits into the carrier in the usual way, being rotated to lock into the chamber by a cam groove in the carrier engaging with a stud on the bolt. Two feed belts are fitted, so that each can carry a different type of ammunition, and feed can be switched instantly from one

belt to the other. It can be seen from this simplified description that there is a comparatively long 'dwell' while the bolt remains closed, which means that a hangfire or slow ignition will still be safely inside the breech when it eventually does fire; also, a misfire will not cause the gun to stop but will be extracted and ejected by the movement of the motor-driven chain. And since all the moving parts are interlinked, there is very precise control of every action inside the weapon, leading to very high reliability. And, finally, the fitting of resistances into the electrical circuit means that the rate of fire can be adjusted precisely as required; this particular model has pre-set adjustment to permit firing single shots, or at 100, 200 or 500 rounds per minute, as desired.

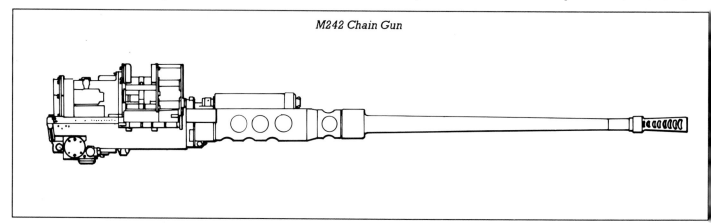

M242 Chain Gun

Specification

Cartridge: 25 x 137 mm

Operating system: Mechanical

Weight, empty: 110.5 kg

Length overall: 2760 mm

Barrel: 2000 mm, 18 grooves, rh

Feed system: Dual, link belt or linkless

Rate of Fire: 100, 200 or 500 rounds/min

Muzzle velocity: ca 1000 m/sec

Manufacturer: McDonnell Douglas, USA

The 25 mm Hughes Chain Gun is the primary armament of the US Army M2 Bradley armoured infantry fighting vehicle.

ASP 30 mm Cannon

USA

The **ASP** (Automatic, Self-Powered) cannon was carefully developed as a combat support weapon which could be used as a substitute for the common .50 heavy machine gun. It is fitted with a dual recoil buffer system so that it can be adapted to any mounting which normally accepts the .50 weapon, and will deliver no greater recoil stress on the mounting that does the machine gun.

The **ASP** is chambered to fire the 30 mm ADEN/DEFA round which is standard throughout NATO and widely used in aircraft cannon, so that ammunition supply will be unlikely to cause problems. moreover, this round, being somewhat lower powered than other 30 mm rounds, also helps to keep the weapon recoil down to the limits demanded.

The **ASP** is gas-actuated, using a rotating bolt mechanism which securely locks the breech during the firing phase of operation.

Feed is by a single belt from the left side, and the short length of the receiver behind the feed point allows it to be mounted in almost any type of turret or cupola and leave ample room behind it. The spade grips and trigger mechanism are similar to those on the .50 machine gun, and operation of the two weapons is similar in many respects, thus easing the training problem.

The **ASP** is manufactured in the USA and also in Britain by Royal Ordnance under licence, these models being fitted to light armoured vehicles in British service.

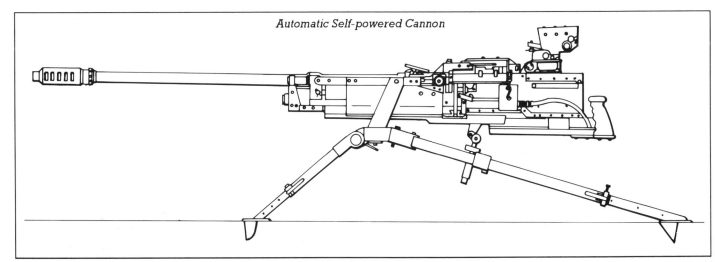

Automatic Self-powered Cannon

Specification:

Cartridge: 30 x 113B ADEN/DEFA

Operating system: Gas, rotating bolt

Weight, empty: 52 kg

Length overall: 2060 mm

Barrel: 1321 mm

Feed system: Disintegrating link belt

Rate of Fire: 450 rounds/min

Muzzle velocity: 820 m/sec

Manufacturer: McDonnell Douglas, USA

The 30 mm ASP cannon in a modified .50 Browning machine gun tripod. The addition of two hydraulic buffers reduces the recoil shock on the tripod and allows this cannon to be used as easily as a machine gun.

M18A1 57 mm Recoilless Rifle

USA

The American **M18A1** is the oldest recoilless weapon still in service, having been introduced in 1945 and used in the Okinawa and Iwojima campaigns in the Pacific. In postwar years numbers were supplied to several countries, and although the weapon has been obsolete in US service for several years it is still used in several South American countries and was copied by the Chinese who probably still hold it in reserve stock.

The **M18A1** is of the small group of weapons known as the 'Kromuskits' from the names of the two designers, Mr Kroger and Mr Musser of the Infantry Section of the US Research & Development Service. It uses a lightweight barrel and a perforated

chamber into which a round of ammunition with a perforated cartridge case is loaded. On firing, about four-fifths of the gas produced by the explosion of the propellant is directed rearwards through vents surrounding the breechblock. The momentum of this light but high velocity gas equals the momentum of the heavier but much slower projectile moving up the bore, so that the two forces balance and the gun does not recoil. In order to keep the bore resistance to a constant figure and also relieve stress on the thin barrel, the driving band of the shell is pre-engraved and has to be fitted into the rifling grooves when the round is loaded.

The weapon is usually fired from a

slightly modified .50 machine gun tripod, though it can easily be fired from a man's shoulder.

The standard ammunition for this gun consists of a high explosive fragmentation shell for anti-personnel use and a shaped charge shell for anti-tank engagements. The original gun was also provided with a canister shot, a thin steel canister loaded with 133 cylindrical steel slugs. On firing, the canister burst and the slugs were ejected from the gun muzzle in the manner of a shotgun, with an effective range of about 55 metres. Although this was an effective anti-personnel round, it is unlikely that any present-day user finds a need for it.

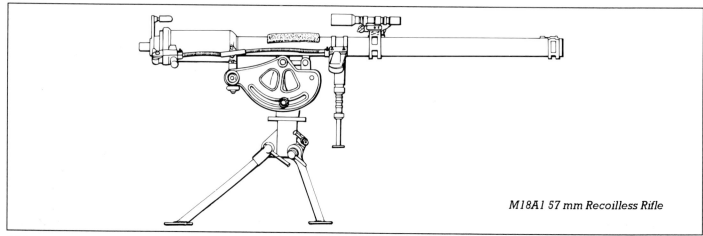

M18A1 57 mm Recoilless Rifle

136

Specification

Manufacturer: Watervliet Arsenal, USA

Calibre of warhead: 57 mm

Weight in firing order: 25 kg

Length: 1564 mm

Maximum range: 4500 m

Muzzle velocity: 365 m/sec

Penetration of armour: 2 mm

Loading the 57 mm recoilless rifle, demonstrating how the loader stays out of the danger triangle of blast behind the breech. This is the original American weapon; the many copies still in use are basically the same, though some have minor refinements.

M40A1 106 mm Recoilless Gun USA

In the years immediately after WW2 the recoilless gun was seen as the only solution to the anti-tank problem; conventional anti-tank guns big enough to damage heavy tanks were far too big to be easily handled on the battlefield, but the light RCL gun and shaped charge shell seemed to be a winning combination. The US Army developed the 105 mm RCL Gun M27 in the 1950s, but this turned out to be an inaccurate and unreliable weapon; it was therefore re-designed, and in order to distinguish the new and improved model it was designated as 106 mm calibre and became the **M40** gun. Although this type of weapon is now outclassed by guided missiles, it is nevertheless cheap and effective and the **M40** is in service with many armies around the world.

The **M40** is a conventional RCL gun, using a venturi in the breech to exhaust a proportion of the propellant gas to the rear so as to balance the momentum of the departing projectile. It is something of an anachronism in using a cartridge case with perforations in the wall, rather than one with a blow-out base. The gun chamber is also perforated, and on firing some four-fifths of the gas generated passes through the case and chamber walls to an external annular space from where it is ejected rearwards through jets encircling the breech. Like all guns of this type there is a large danger area immediately behind the breech and a prominent firing signature of flash and dust.

The **M40** was among the earliest weapons to use the spotting rifle; this is a simple semi-automatic weapon carried in clamps above the barrel and firing a special .50 calibre cartridge with an explosive bullet. The gunner takes aim and presses the trigger, firing a shot from the spotting rifle. Once he has a hit, he maintains his aim, switches to the gun and fires. The trajectories of the spotting round and the main gun round are matched, so that obtaining a hit with the spotter virtually guarantees a hit with the gun.

Three types of ammunition are provided; a shaped charge anti-armour shell; a squash-head anti-armour shell; and an anti-personnel fragmenting explosive shell. The squash-head shell uses a plasticised filling which is deposited on the side of the target and then detonated so as to drive a shock wave through the armour and shake off scabs and needles of steel on the inside of the tank.

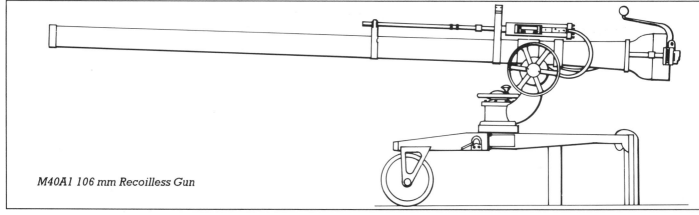

M40A1 106 mm Recoilless Gun

Specification

Calibre of warhead: 105 mm

Weight in firing order: 209.5 kg

Length overall: 3404 mm

Maximum range: 7700 m

Maximum velocity: 503 m/sec

Penetration of armour: 150 mm at 60° angle of impact

Manufacturer: Watervliet Arsenal, USA

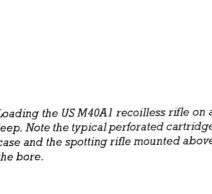

Loading the US M40A1 recoilless rifle on a jeep. Note the typical perforated cartridge case and the spotting rifle mounted above the bore.

M55A4B1 20mm Multiple AA Cannon   Yugoslavia

This is a Yugoslavian-designed equipment which is based upon Oerlikon designs which were purchased several years ago. The gun is derived from the Hispano-Suiza HS 804, while the mounting is based on the Oerlikon GAI-DO1 two-barrel equipment. The Oerlikon design has been extensively modified by fitting a Wankel rotary petrol engine beneath the gunner's seat, driving a hydraulic system to provide power for elevating and traversing. It also drives an air compressor to provide the necessary power for cocking and reloading the three guns. A licence-built copy of an Italian computing optical sight is fitted and there is also a small shield to protect the gunner, who

directs the gun by means of a joystick control.

To engage a target, the guns are cocked and, using an open grid sight, the gunner points the barrels roughly at the target. He enters the estimated speed and range into the sight, after which the sight will automatically calculate the lead and offset to compensate for target motion, correcting this proportionally as the target comes closer. The sight indicates the moment to begin firing, and while the gunner continues tracking and firing his crew change magazines as required to keep up the rate of fire.

The gun can also be used against ground targets, the sight unit having a

separate set of optics for ground use, allowing fire to a horizontal range of 2500 metres.

For transport, the gun has a lightweight two-wheeled trailer which can be rapidly attached to the platform, after which two of the three outriggers are folded up and the whole mounting levered into the carriage. Moving from travelling to firing position or vice versa takes less than one minute.

Ammunition provided for use with this equipment includes high explosive/incendiary, armour-piercing/incendiary, armour-piercing and practice projectiles, all of which can be supplied with or without a tracer element.

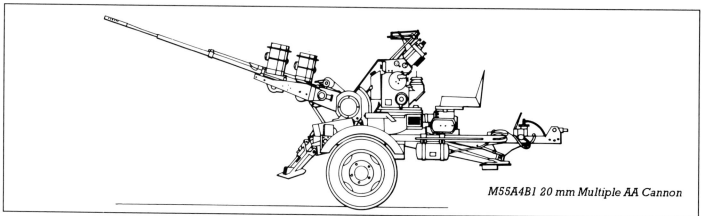

M55A4B1 20 mm Multiple AA Cannon

Specification

Cartridge: 20 x 110 mm

Operating system: Blowback

Weight, empty: 4 kg (gun);   1150
kg (complete equipment)

Length overall: 2207 mm gun; 4.30 m
complete equipment

Barrel: 1400 mm

Feed system: 60-round drum

Rate of Fire: 700 rounds/min per gun

Maximum range: 5500 m

Muzzle velocity: 850 m/sec

**Manufacturer: Federal Supply Bureau
Yugoslavia**

*The Yugoslavian M55A4B1 anti-aircraft
equipment in firing order. The engine
beneath the gunner's seat provides power
for elevation and traverse, and the hydraulic
controls and sighting system are between the
gunner and his three guns.*

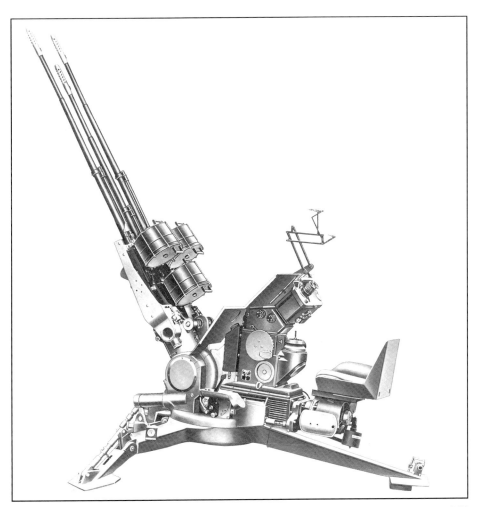

Hand Grenades

Hand Grenades are the Infrantryman's pocket artillery, providing a useful blast and fragmentation effect to disrupt a sudden attack or clear out a confined space such as a room or bunker which would be unwise to enter. They are also provided for making quick smoke screens in order to hide some tactical manoeuvre or blind an enemy while a discreet retirement is being made. Explosive grenades come in two types - offensive and defensive, the difference lying in the spread of fragments. Where the thrower is safely behind cover he can throw a defensive grenade which showers the area with lethal fragments, since he can duck behind his cover and be safe. If, on the other hand, he is running forward in an assault, he wants a grenade which gives a powerful blast effect but keeps its fragments in a small area so as not to endanger the thrower as he runs forward. So, offensive grenades have small fragments which are lethal up to about 5 metres radius but after that soon lose their velocity and become less dangerous. One solution to this is to have a standard offensive grenade made of plastic, for zero fragments but lots of blast, and a cast iron sleeve which you can slip over it to provide fragments if you need them.

An Austrian Hg77 grenade; the body is of plastic, ribbed to give a better grip, and is lined inside with 5500 steel balls. Inside this is 75 grammes of high explosive. The fuze gives a delay of four seconds after pulling out the safety pin and releasing the firing lever.

Top Right: The French F1 grenade is another plastic container with preformed fragments forming an inside layer. Note the shape of the safety pin; a straight pull will not remove it accidentally, it has to be grasped, twisted and then pulled to get it free.

Below: The Spanish M5 grenade, showing that two-thirds of the space is taken up by the fuzing. This grenade is unusual in having a one second safety delay after throwing, impact action irrespective of which way it lands, and a self-destruction device which detonates it after six seconds if the impact fuze fails for any reason.

Below Right: The Spanish M6, a much simpler device than the M5, has an ABS plastic casing covering a thick layer of several hundred steel balls set in a matrix of resin surrounding the filling of high explosive. The fuze mechanism screws into the top and the detonator extends down into the centre of the explosive.

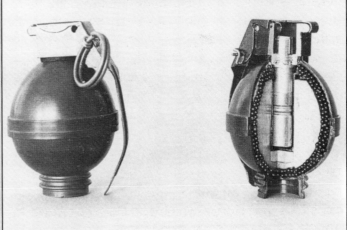

Glossary

ACLOS: Automatic Command to Line of Sight.

CALIBRE: The internal diameter of a weapon's barrel.

COMPUTING SIGHT: A sight which can be programmed with the direction and speed of a moving target.

DISCARDING SABOT: A projectile which is of smaller diameter than the calibre of the gun, made up to the correct diameter by means of a lightweight plastic or metal sleeve or 'sabot'.

ERA: Explosive Reactive Armour.

FOLLOW-THROUGH GRENADE: A warhead with a shaped charge and, behind it, a small projectile.

HESH: High Explosive, Squash Head. See 'Squash-Head'.

IFF: Identification, Friend or Foe.

MCLOS: Manual Command to Line of Sight.

MILLIMETRIC WAVE: A type of radar using a very short wavelength which is close to the optical spectrum.

PRECURSOR CHARGE: A small shaped charge in the extended probe tip of an anti-tank warhead which detonates any explosive reactive armour.

PRIMARY CARTRIDGE: A shotgun-type cartridge in the tail of a mortar bomb.

SACLOS: Semi-Automatic Command to Line of Sight.

SECONDARY CARTRIDGE: A container of propellant explosive attached to the tail of a mortar bomb to give additional propulsive gas.

SHAPED CHARGE: An explosive charge which has the face opposite the target hollowed out into a cone and lined with metal. Also called 'Hollow Charge', 'Neumann Effect' and 'Monroe Effect'.

SPIGOT MORTAR: A weapon in which the 'barrel' is simply a heavy steel rod, and the projectile has a hollow tail which slips over the rod.

STAND-OFF DISTANCE: The distance away from the armour at which a shaped charge must be detonated so as to allow time and space for the shaped charge jet to develop into the correct form for penetration.

SQUASH-HEAD: An explosive charge made of plastic explosive which, when fired at a target, is deposited on to the target like a poultice. Also called HE Plastic (HEP) by US forces.

TANDEM SHAPED CHARGE: Two shaped charges, one behind the other, arranged so as to fire in rapid succession.

THERMAL IMAGING: Detection and recognition of targets by detecting the infra-red emissions from it due to its heat.

THRUST VECTOR CONTROL: A method of steering a missile by varying the direction of the rocket thrust relative to the axis of the missile.

VENTURI: A nozzle which contracts and then expands; gas passing through such a nozzle is accelerated as it passes the constricting point.